LIFELINES

A Guide to Writing Your Personal Recollections

Evelyn Nichols and Anne Lowenkopf

BETTERWAY PUBLICATIONS, INC.
WHITE HALL, VIRGINIA

Published by Betterway Publications, Inc.
P.O. Box 219
Crozet, VA 22932
(804) 823-5661

Cover design and photograph by Susan Riley
Typography by Park Lane Associates

Library of Congress Cataloging-in-Publication Data

Nichols, Evelyn
    Life-lines : a guide to writing your personal recollections /
Evelyn Nichols and Anne Lowenkopf.
        p. cm.
    Includes index.
    ISBN: 1-55870-137-0 : $6.95
    1. Autobiography. I. Lowenkopf, Anne N.   II. Title
CT25.N52 1989
808'.06692--dc20
                                  89-36141
                                      CIP

Printed in the United States of America
0 9 8 7 6 5 4 3 2 1

To our families: those who have gone before, those who are still to come, and those who share our love and the adventure of living.

Contents

PART III: THE WRITING

The Book in Your Life

Have you ever said, "What I've been through; what I've seen in my lifetime! If I could only write!" Well, you can.

This book has been designed to help you. With it, you can embark on an adventure in which you will rediscover the past and touch the future with your words.

It may be a voyage of self-discovery or a search for your own roots. You may want to share your life experiences or provide your children or grandchildren with information about their heritage. You will find this guide flexible enough to suit your particular needs.

A few generations ago families lived close together and spent a lifetime in the same community. People really knew each other. There was less need to put a story on paper. Everyone who mattered knew it already.

But the world has changed. Many of us are separated from our parents, children, and grandchildren by a continent or an ocean. Time spent with our loved ones is precious and short. There is little opportunity for unhurried reminiscences and shared intimacies. Most of us live out our lives without ever sharing our deepest selves. And those who come after never really know us.

So much human experience is lost forever. It doesn't have to be; you can pass yours on. All you need is the conviction that your life matters.

Autobiography and biography are the oldest form of story telling. Even today in the age of television, computers, and space travel, real life stories have power to excite interest and hold an audience.

Why do we want to know about each other? We aren't really all that different. You might expect that the life history of a butterfly with its extraordinary patterns of metamorphosis would be more interesting than another go-round of boy meets girl or girl meets job.

How to explain this fascination with our own kind? Perhaps it is that reading about other people helps us understand ourselves. We see our own emotions and ideas reflected in them and we feel less alone. We discover the possibilities of human behavior, investigate the results of taking roads we turned away from. Through them we vicariously experience passions and enterprises forbidden and unavailable to ourselves.

People's lives are a road map, a yardstick, a how-to or how-not-to book, a short-term reincarnation, a vital resource. Everyone's life history is important because we can never learn enough about what it means to be human.

An American tourist in Sweden, visiting her ancestral town, came upon a manuscript of her family history dating back to the 13th century. She sent copies of the English translation to her fellow descendants, now numbering in the hundreds and spread across the nation, and those hundreds of Swedish Americans were strengthened by pride in family and by a sudden awareness of their personal connection to the historic past.

Can you imagine how astonished the people who wrote that history would have been if they knew their stories were to survive the centuries and travel across the ocean to an undiscovered continent?

You don't know and you can't know how many lives your own story will enrich. In a way it's like a message tucked in a bottle and thrown into the sea, to be read and thrown back again to find its way to someone else. Who will discover it? How will they use what you have written? How many lives will your story touch?

Part I
The Book in Your Life

I

Getting Started

You don't need special talent; if you can tell your story you can write it.

Getting started is always the hardest part. It requires discipline to set aside time to write. Some people work best in the morning, some in the evening. You may do your best writing in the middle of the night when sleep eludes you and the rest of the world is quiet.

Choose your best time. Once the memories begin to flow, their impetus will carry you forward. The process will be exciting as well as rewarding. But don't kid yourself, like anything worth doing, this is work and requires a commitment of time and energy. Establish your own routine and stick to it.

If you use handwriting, it *must* be legible. It's better to type, most convenient if you can use a word processor. With both handwriting and typing be sure to double space and leave wide margins.

Some people have tried taping their memoirs, and it may seem easier to begin with. But once the notes are on tape, locating a particular one becomes so troublesome that developing stories from the material often ends in frustration.

Unless you're lucky enough to be using a word processor, store your answers in a looseleaf notebook or file folders. Label the folders or make separate sections in the notebook to match the main headings in this book, and store your answers, additional notes, and the stories themselves as you write them.

You may find it best to stick to one period because one incident calls up another, and enthusiasm for that time in your life builds on itself. But there are no hard and fast rules; skip around if that's how your mind works. At this point, you just want to pin down memories.

Once you start, write what comes to mind without censoring. Don't worry about spelling, grammar, or style; they will come later. For now, you don't want to stop the flow of your thoughts and feelings. This is your first draft. You will fill in details later. Part III will help you turn this material into stories, and to revise, rewrite, and organize what you write.

As your stories emerge, you will begin to see patterns, gain new insights. The actors in your life will take on different dimensions. You may see your parents and children in a new light, and discover things about yourself you never realized. You will uncover memories you didn't know existed and recall long forgotten moments.

Have the courage to examine the painful as well as the happy times. You may be writing for your family, but every once in a while something will come up that you need to write just for you. Express your true thoughts and feelings. Remember, you're in the room alone with yourself, and you don't need to show what you write to anyone. But you could surprise yourself; some day you might share that story to help someone you love through a painful experience.

Above all, be yourself. Allow your loved ones to meet the real you. Your experiences, your perspective, you yourself are unique. Your story is a gift that no one else can make.

2

Introducing You, the Author

Some people can plunge head first into a project. But there are those of us who need to build a little platform that serves as a springboard. For personal histories, it can be a statement of intent, a way of introducing yourself to yourself, a starting point.

Building a platform can take a number of different forms but perhaps the simplest way is to start out with your name. Then answer the question, why have I decided to write a personal history? What's pushing me? What do I hope to accomplish? What do I need to say about myself and my life before I start digging in my memory?

The following is an example of one person's starting point.

INTRODUCING MYSELF

I'm Edith Helen Brown Kellog Lukas. Yes, they're all me. Each name represents a different time in my life. Together they make up the person I am now.

There have been plenty of ups and downs, but I think I've been lucky, looking back there seem to have been more ups than downs. Or maybe the troubles and hardships seem to fade with the passage of time.

My most recent promotion has been to Medicare. My health has been good till now and I hope I won't be calling on it much. When I retired from teaching ten years ago, sixty-five seemed a long way down the road. It has arrived much faster than I expected. When I look in the mirror, I see a woman who might be in her late fifties. My hair is still mostly black, although the gray is coming through faster now. I still wear the glasses I started to need for reading when I was forty. Only now they're bifocals and I wear them all the time.

And I weigh a few pounds more than I'd like to admit. But people say I look younger than my age. Do they say that to everyone?

As far as I'm concerned, sixty-five is just a number. If I had to pick a time, I'd say that on the inside I feel about forty, mature enough to have lost my shyness and insecurities, young enough to feel competent, confident and attractive.

I do become aware of my age when I realize I get winded climbing hills, forget my best friend's birthday or the name of my favorite author. But I still find life exciting. I have two grown children and three grandchildren. I'm in my second marriage and my third career.

When my about-to-be husband and I approached the church where our minister friend was waiting to marry us in a private ceremony in his office, we saw the subject of next Sunday's sermon on the bulletin board. In those moveable two-inch plastic letters, we read:

> *Grow old along with me*
> *The best is yet to be —.*

We're convinced that quote from Robert Browning was intended for us, although our friend Tony assured us that his sermon had been planned long before our sudden decision to marry. Was that message just coincidence? Serendipity? Synchronicity? Who knows? That was four years ago, and we believe the best is right now. Today.

Why am I writing about myself? I'm not sure — it just feels good. I don't expect to produce a masterpiece. Maybe I want to pass on the things I've experienced and what I've learned along the way. That's the teacher in me.

Or maybe this is a way to tell my kids things I haven't had the chance, or maybe the courage to say directly. No matter how we love them, we can't always speak to our children. Someday my children or their children will be ready to hear. And this will be there, waiting for them.

3

Interviewing You, the Author

A blank page or a blank screen can be a numbing sight no matter how many stories you have to tell or how eager you are to tell them. What's needed is a little outside energy to get you over that first daunting hurdle by focusing your thoughts on what you know. Part II with its memory-stimulating questions does just that. It is designed to be your between-covers, personal interviewer. By the time you've laughed all over again, loved all over again, cried all over again, raged all over again, been scared all over again, cheered all over again, you'll be so busy writing, you'll have forgotten you don't know how.

Part II will help you focus on the important phases of your life in an entertaining and relaxed fashion. You can control the interview yourself by going to the sections that most interest you. Don't feel that you have to read or answer all the questions in a section at one time. And certainly you shouldn't feel obliged to read the sections in chronological order.

What part of your life interests you the most? That is your starting place, whether it's one of the sections on the teen years or on Mid-Life Joys and Crises. Read the questions, and as bits of memory begin to surface note them down for future use. On the other hand if you have no idea where to start or what you want to say, begin skimming the sections of questions. It won't take long to discover portions of your life that are begging to be written about — your life's peaks and pits. Begin writing in response to the questions. Some answers will be only a couple of words, some a sentence, a paragraph, a page. Ignore the questions that don't apply but linger over those that can evoke a whole story or more.

While you're responding to one question, other unrelated flashes of memory may come to mind. Jot them down; they'll come in handy later. Putting your memories down on paper in some form . . . any form . . . is the most important part of the process. In the beginning what you write doesn't have to be ordered or patterned. A word or a phrase may do just as well as complete sentences.

As you read the questions, let yourself feel what it was like then. What memories flash into awareness? They might be of a person, place, event, or just a feeling. Try to recapture the essence of the memory, even if the details are blurred.

Use *all* your senses, the smells and sounds as well as how it looked and felt. Picture yourself in the incidents you are remembering. What do you see? Where are you? Who are you with? What are you doing? Can you hear a neighbor talking? A sibling? What is he/she saying? Are there any animals in the scene? Enter into the memory and let it carry you.

As soon as you begin seeing scenes in your mind, remembering whole incidents, put down the book and start writing. It is better to start on a story while the rush of memory and enthusiasm is at full force than wait until you have answered all the questions in a section. When you get stuck for more material go back to the questions for more stimulation.

Your one-word and other short responses to the questions you answered before you started may add to your story. If they don't, keep them safe; eventually you are going to need them, and it may be that as you look at them again at some later date more details and other related memories will surface to add to your original response.

It would be a pity to confine yourself to chronological order in your writing. If when you are writing about your childhood, an incident that happened years later in married life comes to mind, try tucking the incident as an aside into your story, just as you would if you were talking to a friend. And while you are describing the incident you may want to turn to the sections on marriage for assistance.

The sections of questions are a resource for you. Make use of them again and again. A memory that resisted your first meeting will pop up during a second reading or the third or fourth time around.

This is an exploration. See what comes of it. Your memories will flow more readily, and you will have more fun, if you tackle the questions in the spirit of adventure. Don't worry about the days when nothing seems to come at all. The process of remembering is a mysterious business. Sometimes what is going on in your daily life triggers memories with one past incident tumbling the next domino fashion, other times daily life jams up the process altogether, and your past will seem an absolute blank. Don't worry about the blank periods, and don't strain at remembering. The more you strain, the blanker your past will seem — such is memory's perversity.

After some chores, a shower, a walk, another day, come back to the questions again. Notice how different seasons, different holidays, different clusters of friends and associates affect your response to the questions so that those that seemed meaningless and unproductive in July suddenly become evocative at Christmas. Persistence over time will win through for you. Once the process of remembering begins, it will strengthen and grow more vivid and specific with regular use. And you will be experiencing the joys of time travel.

Part II
The Interviews

4

Your Early Childhood

Most people have no conscious recollection of the time before they were three. But we all carry the imprint of those years upon our personalities. These questions will help you recover those hidden memories. Sometimes you'll just get a feeling, not a clear image. Go with the feeling and see where it leads.

When were you born? In what city and state? Were you born in the hospital? At home? By natural childbirth? Caesarean? Were you baptized? Circumcised? Are there any special stories connected with your birth?

How old were your parents when you were born? Were you their first child? Who was there before you?

Let yourself feel what it was like to be very small. What is your earliest memory? Is it a face? A voice? A feeling?

Describe the first home you remember. Did it seem big to you? Can you remember how the outside looked? What rooms can you visualize? What did the couch look like? Were you sleeping in a crib or a bed? What kind of stove did your mother cook on? Did you have a high chair?

Picture yourself at play outdoors. What do you see? Where are you? Who are you with? What are you doing? Can you hear a neighbor talking? A sibling? What is he/she saying? Are there any animals in the scene? Enter into the memory and let it carry you.

Picture a rainy day indoors. Can you smell food? Describe your surroundings. What are you doing? Where is your mother? Do you remember anyone with you?

Did you have a security blanket? A teddy bear? Any other special or beloved toy?

Do you remember being held? Cuddled? Nuzzled? Bounced on a knee? Tossed in the air?

What was your mother like in those days? Did you ever bring her a flower? A bug? What did the two of you do together?

What about your father? Did you have special times with him?

Can you remember your brothers and sisters? Were they nice to you? Did they tease you? Pinch you? Play with you?

Try to tell about these times from the point of view of the child you were. Do you think you were happier or less happy than most children you knew? Richer or poorer? Did you feel like a success? A failure?

How was your childhood different from that of today's children? What about it would you like to give to the children of this generation? What would you like to spare them?

What would you change about your childhood if you could?

If there were one day, one season, you could live over again, which would it be?

5

Your Schooldays

"Schooldays, schooldays, dear old golden rule days . . .". Were they?

What is your earliest memory of school? Was it a private school? A parochial school? Public school? Was it the same school all your friends were going to? Did you know anyone there before your first day of class? Were you dreading school or looking forward to it?

Where was your school? What did it look like? How did you get there? Who took you? Try to remember looking at that building the first time you entered it. Were you holding onto your mother's hand?

Can you recall the classroom? Did you feel comfortable on that first day? Were your classmates strangers? How many of them were there? Were you frightened? Triumphant?

What did your teacher look like? Was she/he nice? Interesting?

What did you wear? What was your favorite outfit? Did you have to wear a uniform? How did you feel about it? Do you remember being uncomfortably warm or cold in school? Did you feel good about your clothes? Did you care about clothes then?

Were boys and girls in the same classes? Were they separated by seating? Were they allowed to play together? Do you remember note passing? Did you get caught? Were you full of mischief at school? Serious and well behaved?

Were there minority kids in your school? How did they make out? How did you feel about them? Do you think they had a better time or worse time than minority kids today? Were you one of them? How was that for you?

We hear about the "golden days of childhood." Do you remember them that way? Did you have many friends? Any enemies?

Did you know a schoolyard bully? Tattletale? Teacher's pet?

Did the teachers like you? Were they indifferent to you? Have it in for you?

Did you have a favorite teacher? What made this teacher so special?

Did you have a teacher you hated? Were scared of? Try to describe how you felt.

What teacher did you learn the most from? Was it about a specific subject? Can you remember the excitement of being challenged mentally?

Which subjects most interested you? Did you like to read? Tell about some of your favorite books. Was there a subject you weren't good at?

What games did you play at recess? Were they seasonal? In your school, did boys play with boys and girls play with girls?

In general how did you do with the other kids at school? Did you enjoy them? Were you a leader? A follower? A loner?

Who was your best friend? What did you do together? Did you pal around with other kids at school? Can you describe the feeling of comradeship? Were you ever jealous of your friend? What would happen when a stranger would try to enter your group?

Have you kept in touch with any of your schooldays friends?

Did you have to miss school often? Why? Were you frequently late? In general did you enjoy going to school?

Everyone has a few special memories of grade school, triumphs or tragedies, highs or lows. Share a few of yours.

AFTER SCHOOL — HOME LIFE

Where did you live? Tell about your home. Describe your neighborhood. How far away was your nearest neighbor? Was your family on friendly terms with the neighbors? How about you?

Was Mother there when you came home from school? Were you a latchkey kid? What kind of after school snacks did you have?

What did you do after school? Who were your friends? Where did you play? Was there plenty of space to run and climb? If you kids made noise did it bother the grownups?

Did you play games: jacks, jumprope, hide and seek, giant steps, statues, hopscotch, red light-green light, pussy in the corner, marbles, baseball, stickball, boxball, basketball, football, stoopball, kites? Which was your favorite? Which were you good at? Bad at? Can you remember the kids you played with? Who was the most fun? Was there one you didn't like? Did your parents ever play with you?

Did you play: house, dolls, board games, cops and robbers, soldiers, cowboys and Indians, aliens and spacemen, video games?

In your neighborhood was there a time when you kids began "playing doctor"? Where were you when it happened? Can you remember the excitement? Were you disappointed with what you saw? Did the thought of doing it behind your parents' backs add to the fun? If your parents had discovered you would they have been very angry?

When you became a parent how would you have felt to have walked in on such a scene?

Did you collect: butterflies, fireflies, frogs, tadpoles, stamps, coins, paper dolls, baseball cards, popsicle sticks, trains, toy soldiers?

Were there chores after school and little time for play? What about your friends — did they have to help out too? What were your jobs? Did you like them? Were you proud of helping? Did your parents make you feel good about your contribution? Were they nags? Did you feel resentful?

Was there a family pet? What was it? Who took care of it? What part did it play in your life?

When did you have to come in from play? What did you do? Chores? Schoolwork? What did you do on rainy days?

What did you do in the summertime?

Did you ever go to camp? Boy/Girl Scout Camp? Day camp? Sleep-away camp? Music camp? Tennis camp? Overweight camp? Computer camp? Did you like it? Were you lonely? What was worst about the first day? What was best about the last week? Did you have a crush on a counselor? What were some of the crazy things you did?

What happened when you got sick? Very sick? Broken bones?

Did you have an encounter with death during your childhood? A person? A pet? How was it treated in your family? How did it affect you? Did the loss hurt much? Were you afraid of dying?

Was your mother a good cook? Were family meals fun? Were there quarrels at the table? Heavy silences? Laughter? Did you and your siblings kick each other under the table? Secretly feed the dog? Were you made to eat more food or kinds of food you didn't want? How about table manners — were they emphasized?

Were there after-dinner treats: cake and milk, fruit and nuts . . .? Fun activities like: roasting chestnuts, popping corn, making fudge, pulling taffy, baking cookies . . .?

What did you do in the evenings? Homework? Was schoolwork emphasized in your house? Were your grades considered important? Were you ever punished for bad grades? Were you ever called stupid in connection with your schoolwork or chores?

Did you listen to the radio in the evening? Alone or with the family?

What did the grownups do in the evenings: read, play cards, dance, sing, make music, listen to the Victrola or radio or television? What books did they read? What music did they listen to? Were your family "enjoyers"? Did they laugh at the comedians and shout at games, get involved in the dramas, talk excitedly about the news? Or did they listen impassively?

Did they have company over? Frequently? Family or friends? How did you feel about it?

What did your mother do in the evenings by herself? Your father? Did the family gather together in the evening? In what part of the house? Describe a typical evening.

Did your parents ever go out in the evening? To parties? To the movies? To theatre and concerts? Can you remember any of the performers they talked about?

How were they dressed? How did you feel about the way they looked? Did you mind their leaving? Who took care of you?

How did the family celebrate birthdays? Is there one that stands out in your mind? Do you remember some of your birthday presents?

When did you have to go to bed? Was there a definite time? Did you try to stretch it? Was bedtime a conflict between you and your parents? Did you read in bed? Under the covers? Did you have pillow fights? Pajama parties?

The bathroom scene: Did your family have an indoor bathroom? More than one? Did you and your siblings bathe together? Get in trouble for having water fights in the tub? Or did you shower?

How about outhouses, or bathrooms shared with other families? Was there a time when you had to bathe in cold water? Had to heat the bath water on the stove?

Did you ever watch your daddy shave? Did you ever watch your mother get dressed?

Did your parents let you children see them without their clothes? Did your parents ever take a bath with you? Can you remember when you were no longer allowed to run around naked?

Were you taught to be ashamed of showing your body? What degree of undress was permitted in your family? How did you feel about it? How do you feel about it now?

Were you frequently in trouble? Practically never in trouble? What did you do that made your parents angry? How did they punish you? Were you frightened of them? Did you enjoy testing the limits, seeing how much you could get away with? When did you enjoy your parents? Do you think your parents enjoyed you? How did they show their feelings?

Neighborhood memories: the grocery store, shopping for clothing. Deliverymen: iceman, milkman, bakery man, vegetable man, rag man.

Can you remember a neighbor who was particularly nice to you? Gave you cookies? Let you play in his/her yard? What was special about the yard? Try to describe your feelings about the neighbor. Did you tell your parents or was that a special secret?

Was there any childhood experience, person, or event that had a powerful impact on you?

Did any adult when you were growing up fondle you in a way that made you uncomfortable? What did you do about it? Could you tell your parents? Did it happen once or twice or more frequently? Did you ever see a flasher? Where were you? Were you frightened, or did you think it was dumb? Can adults protect their children from that kind of assault?

What was the best time you can remember having as a child? The worst time?

Do you think some of your adult traits were molded in childhood? What trait began in childhood that you now are most proud of? Least proud of?

6

Your Teen Years

These are the years of growth spurts, raging hormones, awareness of our own bodies and those of the opposite sex. Here is a chance to do a replay of your own adolescence.

Think about yourself as a teenager. What was going on in the world at that time? War? Depression? Prosperity? How did this affect you or your family? Did you think about it much at the time?

Picture yourself at that age. Were you tall, short, thin, fat, pimply, gorgeous? How did you feel about the way you looked?

What did you think of yourself? How did you think other kids saw you? How about the adults around you?

How were you most of the time? Excited? Running around like crazy? Angry? Feeling very much part of the gang? Focused on a single friend? Was there a wonderful sense of loyalty and bonding? Did you feel life opening up before you?

Did you feel left out? Alone? Frightened? Angry? Jealous? Did you feel different from the other kids? When did that start? Was there no one to talk to about it? What do you think was wrong?

Were you bored? Did you hate everything you did? Was there something you wanted to do but couldn't? Did you know what you wanted?

Describe your room. If you didn't have your own room where did you keep your things? Where did you sleep?

What part did religion play in your life at this age?

At what age did you become aware of your own sexuality? How did it affect your behavior?

What was your attitude toward the opposite sex at this time? Were they something to be conquered? Something you needed to establish your own status with your friends? With yourself? Were they something unknown and wonderful you wanted but couldn't approach comfortably? Did you feel at ease around them? Did you think of "the opposite sex" or were they persons to you — some you liked, some you didn't like?

How did you act?

Was the other sex interested in you?

Did you still feel most comfortable with your friends of the same sex? Did you plot and joke together about romantic and sexual feelings?

Did all this cause a conflict with you and your parents? Were you comfortable about your sexual feelings? Did they make you feel more connected to the world about you or more isolated?

Were they connected to the beginnings of "nesting," of wanting to start a family of your own? Or were they part of adventure, romance? Was the thought of domesticity repugnant?

What kind of sex education did you receive? How did it influence you? Would you hope others had the same sexual background you did?

Was alcohol part of your teen years? Drugs? How did getting high make you feel?

In the beginning was obtaining it more fun than consuming it? Were alcohol and drugs something you did mostly with the same sex or with the opposite sex? Did they play a part at school dances? Neighborhood parties? Beach parties?

Did alcohol, cigarettes, or drugs allow you to feel more at ease with the opposite sex? Did it become part of your dating pattern? Part of the preliminaries of sex?

Were you allowed to date? Did you date without your parents' permission?

What was your first date like? How did it come about? Who was it? Where did you go? What did you do? Was it anything like you expected? How was it different?

What did you usually do on a date? How did you finance your dating?

Do you remember your first kiss? Where were you? Did you have a "steady" or lots of different dates? Did you smooch, neck, pet, make out, go all the way???

Was there one person who was really special to you? Was that person always an ideal, a kind of fantasy you never really knew? Did that person become close, a friend and companion as well as a source of a new kind of excitement?

How did you spend your leisure time? Did you have a car? Could you repair it? Where did you go with it?

Did your boyfriend have a car? Your girlfriend? Most of the kids?

Did you get an allowance? How much? How would this be translated to modern-day money? What were you expected to use it for? Carfare? School supplies? Movies? Your own clothes? Was it enough?

Were you allowed to choose your own clothes? Were your

clothes a source of conflict between you and your family? Did you have to wear hand-me-downs? Whose? Did your mother ever sew clothes for you? Did you like to wear them? Could you tell your mother how you felt? Did you and your siblings trade clothes? Who thought the way you dressed was important, you or your family?

Describe your favorite outfit. How did you usually dress? How long did you have to wait for your first pair of long pants/high-heeled shoes?

Do you remember shopping with your mother? Did she haggle about price? Was price no object?

Did you have a job? What was it? How did you feel about working? How much were you paid? What did you do with your earnings? What was your first important purchase?

What did you want to be when you grew up? What did your family want you to be?

How important were home and family to you during your early teens? Did you have responsibilities at home? What were they? How did you feel about them?

Were you angry? Resentful? Could your parents make you crazy? Feel guilty? Mostly affectionate? Did you feel they were there for you if you needed them? Could you talk to them?

Describe your brothers and/or sisters. Where were they and what were they doing during those years? What were they like? How did you get along with each other?

What was your relationship with your mother, your father, at this time? How did you feel about them on a day-to-day basis? Were they still making rules for you? Did you obey them? Did you feel they were fair? How do you feel now?

What were the rules and restrictions in your family? Could

you come and go as you pleased or did you have to account to your parents? Do you think you had too much freedom? Too little?

What was your mother's role during your adolescent years? Could you talk to her? How about your father? Were you able to be honest with him? How did you feel about your parents? Were you proud of them? Did they bore you? Did you and your parents share interests and beliefs?

Were you living up to your family's expectations? How did you feel about their expectations?

Did you have secret thoughts you couldn't share with anyone? Could you talk about them now?

Was there one member of the family with whom you were especially close? Who was it? Describe the relationship. Relate some incidents involving that person.

Who was your first love? How old were you when you met? How did the experience affect you?

Was "the gang" just some other teenagers you ate hamburgers and went to the movies with or was it a real organization? Did you want to be part of it? Did you have to be part of it? Did you feel safer because of your gang? Less safe? Did you come into conflict with other gangs? With the police? Your parents? What was your position in the gang? Do you sometimes miss the camaraderie?

Some very important and successful people had little formal education. What about you? Where did your schooling end? Why did it end?

Do you appreciate your freedom from the restrictions of formal education? When you are talking to a person with a university degree do you sometimes feel they're all theory and no common sense?

If you are self-educated, how did you do it? How did you feel about not going to high school? Describe your life during those years.

Do you sometimes feel defensive in the presence of formally educated people? Do you occasionally congratulate yourself on having escaped a formal education? At times do you wish you had been able to finish high school?

Do you remember yourself as mostly a loving, angry, confident, or frightened teenager? Did you enjoy those years or were they hard for you? Were you happier or less happy than most of your friends? Than your children during their teens?

If you could change one thing in that part of your life, what would it be? What would you like to pass along to the teens of this generation?

7

Religious and Ethnic Traditions

There was a time when Americans tried to forget their origins and assimilate into the mainstream of America. It took Alex Haley's *Roots* to show us that religious and ethnic variety *are* the American culture.

What was the first contact you can remember with your religion: Prayer, feasts, fasting, ceremonies, church . . .?

When were you first aware that you were Protestant, Jewish, Catholic, Moslem, Secular Humanist, Buddhist, Hindu, Navajo . . .? Was it something you saw, felt? Did someone tell you? Who told you? How did you feel?

What was your religious training? Did you receive formal instruction? Daily? Weekly? Never? How did you feel about it? Did you like the person who gave you instruction?

Did your family pray? Together? Before or after meals? At bedtime? Were the prayers in English?

Did the family observe religious holidays? How? Were they festive or serious?

Were there religious images and objects in your house? How did they make you feel?

Were there things in your religion that you *had* to do? Some you couldn't do? Customs? Food? Fasting? Dress?

Did you follow the rules? Did you feel good about it? Hate it? Did you love God? Fear God?

Did your friends share your religion? Did some kids tease you about it? Were you ever ashamed of your religion? Did you ever envy your friends' religion? What about it seemed attractive?

Were your family Atheists? Agnostics? Did you feel lucky about not having to go to religious services? Did you feel isolated living in a Christian culture?

When you were little did your family's religious beliefs and customs make you feel warm and secure? Did they make you feel good about yourself? Worried? Scared?

What rituals were special to you as a child? Were you squirmy and restless during services?

Did you turn to prayer in moments of crisis? When you thought you had done something wrong? Did your religion make you feel better?

Did your feelings change during your teen years? What caused the change?

Did you take an active part in religious ceremonies? In the choir? Altar boy? Bar/Bas Mitzvah? Group prayers? Meditation? Group ceremonies? By your own choice or did you have to?

Who were the religious authorities in your childhood? Priest, Minister, Sisters, Rabbi, Swami, Elders, Singer? How did they treat children? Did you love them? Fear them? Some middle ground? Have you ever wanted to thank one of them? Have you ever fantasized telling them off? Did you ever consider becoming a Religious?

Was there a period when religion was more important to you than it is now? Can you remember how you felt then? What did your religious life do for you? What changed — your belief systems, your focus of interest, conflicting demands?

Has religion become more important to you with the years? Did a change in church make the difference? A particular person? Your own development? How do your religious beliefs and feelings help you? How do they fail you?

Do you have moments of strong religious awe? What brings them on? Do you still pray during crisis? Do you have the sense of your prayers being heard?

Does talk of religion make you uncomfortable?

If you belong to an ethnic minority, did it create problems for you? In what areas? Were you ever ashamed of being part of your community? Proud of it? Felt superior because of it? Vacillate in your feelings? Were you even aware that there was another world outside of your tradition?

Describe your favorite ritual or holiday. What was your personal contribution to the festivities? How did you dress up for the holidays? In any special costume? What special objects or customs are associated with this day?

Was there a holiday you hated? What turned you against it?

Describe as many of your traditional holidays and rituals as you can remember. Try to recall the feelings associated with each one. How did they differ? Were any of them fun? Solemn? Festive? Did they involve processions? Food? Music? Dance?

What foods do you remember? How did they smell? How did they look? How did they taste? Which celebration had the best food?

Describe the kitchen while the meal was being prepared. Who was there? Try to capture their mood. What were they doing? Did you help? What were your jobs? Rewards?

8

High School Memories

For most of us high school was the end of childhood and the next step beyond family and neighborhood. It was a critical time of testing, of triumphs and setbacks that prepared us for the adult world.

Where did you attend high school? What was its name? Was your school attractive? How did you get there? How large were your classes? Were there any rules or expectations with regard to dress? Behavior? How did you feel about this? Was there anything special about your school?

What did you think of your teachers? Did you have one or two great teachers? What was great about them? What did they look like? Did you have some really awful teachers? What did they do? How did they affect you?

Which subjects did you like? Are you still interested in them? Was there anything — other than the opposite sex — that intrigued you (inside or outside a high school text)? Did your teachers encourage you to go with it?

What subject didn't you like? Were you simply not interested? Were you afraid because it wasn't coming easily? Or was it the teacher?

What were your grades like? Did you have a brother or sister who always had better grades than you? Worse grades? Were you looking forward to college?

Did you secretly believe you were smarter than most of your friends? Not as smart?

Did your teachers see you as a model student, a rebel, an average student, or were you invisible to them?

How did you see yourself in relation to the other students? Were you popular? Were you a loner? Were you a leader? A follower? Has that pattern continued?

What did the "wild kids" in your school do? Were you one of them? Did you wish you could be? Did you date one of them? Did you want to? Were they exciting? Frightening? Repelling?

Did you smoke? Where? With whom? What brand? Can you remember what you talked about? How did you get the money for cigarettes? What about pot? Did smoking get you in trouble with school authorities?

How about drinking? Where? When? What? How did you get the liquor? Were you ever caught? Do you remember being drunk? At school? When you were driving? What about other drugs?

Did you ever ditch school (cut classes)? What did you do with the time? Were you caught? What happened? Did you or someone you know ever do anything really illegal?

Were you involved in extracurricular activities? Sports, music, drama, clubs? Describe them. Any big moments?

What was the big sport at your school? Describe one of the games.

What about high school dances? Were they fun? How did you dress for them? What did you do for music? Were you a good dancer? Who was your favorite partner? Was there someone you would have liked to dance with but never had the chance to?

Who were your teenage heroes or heroines?

Do you think school prepared you well for the future?

What needed to be changed for you to have benefited more from your high school days?

How do you think high school in your time compares with the schools today? Try to think of at least one way that schools have improved and one way that the schools of your day were better.

Was your father's/mother's job or career secure during your high school years? Did your family have any money problems? How did it affect your life and your plans?

If your family was more affluent than most, did that present a problem? Did you enjoy the power and prestige money gave you?

As high school neared its end did you know what you wanted to do with your life?

What did your high school graduation mean to your family? What did it mean to you?

Do you think of those as the best days of your life?

9

Holidays and Vacation Time

Fun in the sun, parades, picnics, adventure, laughter, relaxation . . . holidays could also be times of family tension and raw nerves. What do you remember?

In your area was Spring Vacation a big deal? Where did the kids go? What did they do? Were you one of them? Did you instigate or go along with the activities?

Did you have a problem with some of what went on? How did you resolve it? Did you enjoy yourself during the Spring Break? Did you ever tangle with the law? With your parents?

If you had to stay home when the rest of your class went off for Easter Week — or any other special occasion — how did you feel about it?

Each year did you look forward to the last day of school? How did you spend summers? At the seashore, the mountains, with relatives, at home, on the streets and corners of your town?

Did you travel? With the family? Abroad?

Did you spend outdoor summers? Camping, fishing, hiking, horseback riding, surfing?

Did you have a summer job? What was it? What was your boss like? Did you return to it every summer?

Why did you work? Because you were interested in the job? Because you had to? To contribute to the family? To have your own money? What did you do with the money?

What about family holidays? In your family who was in charge of the preparations?

How did you feel about those big gatherings? Were they noisy? Formal? Joyous? Crosscut with undercurrents? Did preparing for them make your mother crazy? Did your father grumble about the expense?

Were you ever the flower girl or ring bearer at a wedding?

Did your family make a big deal over festivities? Furious cleaning? Decorations? Cooking? Excited planning? Money no object? New clothes? Did they make the whole family happy? Was it a time of covert backbiting and sniping? A little of both? Did you enjoy it? Did a time come when you stopped enjoying it?

Do you try to continue those traditions in your present life? Does preparing for them make YOU crazy? Does your family follow the same traditions? Do you grumble about the expense?

What was your most enjoyable vacation? The worst dud?

What was your all-time favorite family get-together?

IO

In Those Days

If you grew up in the first half of this century you had experiences that your children and grandchildren can only read about. This is your chance to tell it as you saw it.

What were the fads of your time? Tea dances? Jitterbugging? Rock and Roll? Barbershop quartets?

How did young people dress? Saddle oxfords? Bobby socks? Angora sweater sets? Charm bracelets? Pegged pants? Zoot suits?

How about hair? Crew cuts? Grease? Page boys? Long and straight? Pompadours? Hair nets? Buns? Rats? Blown dry?

Expressions like: So's your old man, the cat's pajamas, marvy, dynamite, twenty-three skidoo, swell, neat, cool . . .

How much did things cost? Movies, a haircut, ice cream, streetcar or bus fare, cigarettes, school supplies, shoes, a dress, suit? Do you remember the price of a loaf of bread? A pound of butter? Other foods? What else comes to mind?

Where did your mother shop for food? How often? On foot? Did she sometimes take you with her? Try to capture the image of the butcher, the grocery, the vegetable store, the fish store, etc. Do you remember the grocery clerk fetching your items? No waiting in lines? Home delivery?

Do you remember choosing live fish or poultry? Did you ever watch a chicken being plucked? Pluck it? An animal you had fed being slaughtered? Describe your feelings.

What part did movies play in your life? Can you remember a few favorite movie stars? Are any of them still around? Do you think movies influenced the way you viewed life? Did you enjoy movies better then than now? Why? Did your family go to Bingo Night?

Do you remember when radio was the major form of entertainment in your home? Did your family listen together? Where? When? What were your parents' favorite programs? What were YOUR favorites? Did you fight with your brothers and sisters over radio shows? Did you mother listen to soap operas in the afternoons? Did you? Which ones?

How important were books in your life? What books were popular? Did anything you read at that time have a powerful influence on you?

Who were your friends? What did you do together? What do you know about those friends now? Are you still in touch with them?

How did you get around? Horse and buggy? Trolley car? Bus? Taxi? Subway? Ferry? Bicycle? Feet? Was it a hardship? Was it fun? Did you and your parents see it differently?

How was the family laundry done? Have you ever hung up a family wash to dry? Remember when it froze on the line? Remember the sound it made flapping in the wind? Did it ever get blown down? Dragged down by a dog?

Did your family have a car? Was getting a car an issue? Who won? Who lost? What were their arguments?

What was the farthest you ever traveled? By train, ship, airplane, some other means? How did it feel? Did you brag about it to your friends? Did you want to travel again?

What about those days do you miss now? What about them makes you feel the "good old days" weren't really that good?

II

Animals in Your Life

Animals are our connection with nature. They satisfy our yearning for love and acceptance. Studies show that stroking a cat or dog lowers blood pressure. Whatever the reason, there is evidence that people who have pets are healthier and live longer.

What did you call your first pet? Remember the way it made you feel? Who gave it to you? What did you name it? Where were you when you first saw it? What did the two of you do together?

Describe your pet, including the way it moved, the foods it liked, sounds it made, and where you kept it.

How old were you at the time? What did your family think of it? Who took care of it?

What was your favorite pet?

Was there a family pet you were jealous of because of the attention and affection it got?

What pet gave you the most trouble?

In your family were dogs fed at the table? Allowed on furniture? Used for hunting? Who did your dad take hunting? You or the dogs or both?

Our pets shower us with unconditional love; they infuriate us; they worry us; they impoverish us; and often they mortify us. We knew a Blue Tick Hound who walked up to a strange woman in a laundromat and lifted his leg to her. What was your most embarrassing moment with a pet?

What pet was most expensive? Most exotic? Hardest to please? Caused the most trouble?

Which was your smartest pet? Do you think dogs are smarter than cats? In your house who bullied whom?

Did you go to obedience school? Who came out best — you or your pet? What did the place, the other pets, pet owners, and the trainer look like?

Have you ever held a cat when it was really scared? Do you remember the first time you tried to stuff a pill down a cat's throat? Do you go to sleep with a cat purring in your arms?

Have you displayed your pet at an animal show? Describe the melee, its sights, sounds, and smells. How did you feel when it was your turn in the ring? How did your pet behave?

What stories do you have about encounters with other people's pets?

Were you always bringing home strays when you were little? Do you remember the phrase, "But, Mama, it's lost!"

Do you still bring home strays? Belong to an animal rescue group? Will you endanger yourself to rescue an animal running loose on the highway?

Did you ever breed a pet and watch it give birth and raise its young? Did one of your pets ever breed at its own whim to your dismay? Did your folks sell the litter?

Have you done some horseback riding? Western or Eastern saddle? What happened the first time you mounted a horse? Did you have a trainer? What were his/her methods? What clothes did you wear and how did you feel in them? Did you groom and care for a horse? Did you do your own saddling up? What was the most intelligent horse you've ridden? The meanest? Have you ever ridden a horse that had a sense of humor? Have you ever raced? Jumped fences? Competed in a horse show? What was your favorite ride?

DOMESTIC ANIMALS

Did you belong to the 4-H club at school? What about vacationing on a farm or ranch?

Have you ever raised chickens? Been chased by an enraged goose? Did you make pets of your poultry? Were they healthy? Good layers? Smart?

Have you ever milked a cow? Describe the feeling of your head in the cow's flank, your hands pulling milk out of her, the smells of milking? What time of day was it? What were you wearing?

What about slopping pigs or helping catch escaping piglets? Have you ever set hives, gathered honey?

WILD ANIMALS

Did you collect bees, bugs, or polliwogs when you were little?

Are you a hummingbird, bluejay, or squirrel feeder? Have you ever rescued a hurt, wild animal?

How many birds have you watched?

Are you a feeder of ducks and raccoons? Have you ever met a swan? A great blue heron? An eagle? Have you ever had a bird nesting where you could watch it raise its young?

What about a dog that insisted on tangling with skunks?

Are you tracking the fate of whales, whooping cranes, condor, wolves?

Have you encountered wild animals on camping trips? Has a coyote band's ululating awakened you? Did you ever catch a glimpse of a bobcat? A fawn and its mother? Heard a cougar scream? Have you had a dog that went after porcupines? What is it like to be mealtime for a tick? Have you ever run into the wrong end of a skunk?

Are you a hunter? Have you ever tried to be a hunter?

What about trips to the zoo or animal parks?

Have you suffered infestations of ants, rats, mice, bees, wasps, fleas, cockroaches, mosquitoes? Who won? How do you feel about spiders?

Do you fish? Freshwater or salt? Describe your skills and the equipment you use. What was the most fish you ever caught? What battle with a fish excited you most? What do you do with your catch? Describe the most disastrous fishing trip you've taken, and then your favorite.

12

Wartime

The twentieth century has been torn by an endless series of wars, many of them involving the United States. Which did you live through? How do you think it affected your country? How did it affect you?

IF YOU WERE IN THE ARMED FORCES

For most men and women this part of their lives was completely alien from what came before and after. Its very routines are strange to those who have never known military service. Be lavish with detail and incident to create a clear picture of that world and how it affected you and to give the experience its proper importance in your life.

TRAINING

Describe the tension of the days surrounding being drafted or your enlistment. Were you proud to join up? Not happy about it but "willing to do your part"? Angry at having your life disrupted? Enraged and disgusted at being forced to take part in a war you thought was immoral? Did you consider "draft dodging"? Know anyone who did?

Was there a branch of the service you really wanted? Is that where you landed? How did the reality compare with what you expected? What was your entering rank?

Describe your day of induction and your first experiences of barracks life. How old were you? Was this your first time away from home? Did you have to abandon the values of your youth?

Did you make friends right away? Was there a camaraderie about barracks life that felt good at the time? Did you feel alien and out of place? Was there no one you could talk to? How much hostility did you run into?

Where were you stationed? Was it very far from your hometown? How did it differ?

What was basic training like? How did you like your officers? Did you make any friends? Any enemies? Describe some of the men in your outfit.

What did you do on your first leave? Did you have a good time? Did you feel lonely? Did you do anything that you wouldn't have done or couldn't have done at home?

STATESIDE

Where were you stationed? Were you transferred often? Did you discover parts of America you'd never known? Were the townspeople friendly? Were there adequate facilities for recreation? Describe the most boring and most exciting parts of your work.

Did you have more authority than in civilian life? Less? Did you feel you were being bossed around more than in civilian life? Did you feel comfortable with or resent military discipline? Did the service make the best use of your abilities? Did it bring out abilities you didn't know you possessed?

Did you worry about your wife and family? Were your worries chiefly financial? How often did you get to see them? Describe a typical leave at home. Did you receive much mail? Did you write home often? Did you open up about what was happening to you in your letters?

Did you still feel like part of your community? How did you look in uniform? Were you proud to be wearing it when you went home? Did the family make a fuss over you? Were you a celebrity in the neighborhood? Was home cooking really better than the mess?

Did your wife (girlfriend) visit you? What kind of accommodations did you find for her? How long could she stay?

Was your wife able to live near or on the base? Did she adapt to being a service wife? Did she help your service career?

Were you seeing more of this country than you would have seen if you hadn't been in the military? What about different kinds of people, men and women of different financial, ethnic, social, and educational backgrounds and coming from different regions? Did you get a broader, deeper feel for the country? Or do you feel the military locked you into a narrow perspective? Did you feel cut off from opportunities for personal growth?

OVERSEAS

Where were you sent? What was it like? How did you feel about being separated from your loved ones? What about the times the mail didn't come through? Family crises? A new baby?

Did you see or experience combat? Were you wounded? Where? Was there quick medical help? Do you still suffer from your injuries?

To your knowledge, did you ever wound anyone? How did you feel about it then? Now?

Looking back, do you still carry the effects of combat? Do you ever dream of combat? Would you want your son or daughter to have those experiences?

Were you engaged in behind the lines work? What about it was routine and boring and what challenging? Did you learn skills you use today?

What part did army buddies play in your life? Did you buddy around with people you didn't really like? Did you have one or two particular friends? What became of them? Do you still know any of them? How do you keep in touch? Have you had friendships in civilian life that are as close?

When you weren't in battle, what was camp life like? Where did you go on leave? Did you see much of the surrounding country? What did you do for R and R? Did you get to know the people? Were you able to travel around much?

Did you see much drinking or drug use? On or off base? How was the distribution managed? How much did it cost? Did your superiors close their eyes to what was going on? How did you feel about it when you first saw what was going on? Did you get sucked into it? How did you feel about it then?

Tell about your unit. What was your particular duty? Did the men in command make you feel secure? Insecure? Did your unit pull together? Did you ever see the face of your enemy?

BEHIND THE LINES

How far behind the lines were you? Did you have the freedom to go sightseeing? Was there an opportunity to meet the people of the area? How did you feel about them? Did you pick up new tastes, new interests?

Was romance part of your life then?

Were your bonds to home life still strong? Did family and friends stay in touch?

What was your job? Did it hold your interest? Was the work load heavy? Bureaucracy maddening? Responsibilities harrowing? Did you handle them well? How did you feel about your place in the chain of command? Describe a typical day. Did you feel your unit was doing a good job?

Were you relieved (did you feel guilty) not to be in combat? How did you feel around men with combat ribbons?

WOMEN IN THE SERVICE

Why did you volunteer? What choices of service did you have? Why did your choice appeal to you? Were you given the assignment you wanted? Was the life harder than you'd expected? How old were you? How did the service differ from life at home? Did you find more or less freedom?

What were the other women in your unit like? Who were your friends? Were they really close? What did you talk about with your buddies: Men? Where to find silk stockings? Food?

Was the discipline difficult for you? Describe some of the women in authority over you.

What was basic training like? Did barracks life agree with you? What was your hardest duty? What did you enjoy most? What was most strange and different? Did it seem like a different world?

Were you an officer? Did you feel comfortable with your new authority? Were you able to find a satisfactory balance between power and warmth?

Who was your best friend in the service? Was making friends easier or more difficult in this new life? Were the women you served with different from those you knew back home?

What did you do in the service? Were you using new skills or those you had already developed in civilian life? Did you find yourself working with men? Higher or lower in rank? Any problems?

Where were you stationed? Was it far from home? How often were you able to visit your family? Were you a celebrity in your hometown? Did military life make you feel estranged and alien when you were home on leave?

How did your parents feel about your being in the service? Did the guys in your hometown still look good to you?

Where did you go on leave? What did you do? Were you dating servicemen? Did rank ever interfere with your dating?

How did you deal with this sudden opportunity for sexual freedom? Was it frightening? Liberating? Did you have a serious love affair? How did it end? Or did it?

Did you go overseas? Where? What was the experience like? Did it give you a taste for travel?

When you were discharged, did you find civilian life better or worse than your life in the service? Did you ever have as much responsibility again? Did you find more or less freedom? Did you have more or fewer worries about money?

If you had it to do over, would you sign up again? Would you want your daughter to go into the service?

COMING HOME

Did you find you had become a different person in the service? How did your community look on your return?

Had your relationship with your parents changed? Did you feel like a stranger in your own family? What about your wife (husband)? Girlfriend? Boyfriend? Civilian chums?

Were the available jobs equal to your new expectations? How did you feel about having to start at the beginning when so many of your peers who stayed home had been able to build successful careers?

When you took off your uniform, did you lose an important degree of authority and status? Did you bring home bad habits? Important skills? Increased self confidence? A stomach full of anger?

How did you feel about your country and your way of life?

IF YOU WERE NOT IN THE SERVICE

If you were a male of military age during one of the major conflicts, what kept you out and how did you feel about not being in uniform? How did your family and friends feel about your civilian status? What was the nature of your work? Were you proud of it? What was your social life like?

Women who did not serve in the military were also deeply affected. Were you one of those who replaced men in factories and on farms? What did the new responsibilities feel like? What about money — did you have more of it than before the war, more control of it? After the war did you resent giving up your work?

Were you a war bride? Did you follow your husband from camp to camp or lose him for months and years? Was this your first experience in managing family finances? How did you cope with taking over responsibilities the man of the family usually handled? What did you enjoy (hate) most?

Did you have children before the war? While your husband was in the service? What was it like to be a "single parent"?

Remember ration books? Sugar, meat, butter shortages? White margarine? Gasoline rationing? Black market steaks? Silk stockings?

What about following the war from radio newscasts? Watching Pathé News? Waiting for letters? Did you ever receive a telegraph from the War Office? How did you handle it?

Were you one of the unmarried, man-hungry women of the war years? Did it make you feel unattractive? Anxious about ever getting married? What was your social life like?

Do you remember the last day of the conflict? Armistice Day? V-E or V-J Day? The end of the Korean or Vietnam War? How did you learn the war was over? Did you celebrate? How did you feel? What were your expectations?

In what ways did the war have a lasting effect on your life?

13

College Days

Football heroes, fraternities, sororities — that was Hollywood's picture of college life before World War II. The G.I. bill opened academic doors to thousands of young men and women who had never dreamed of being able to afford a higher education. Then came the sixties with its strikes and sit-ins. Where did you fit in?

What college/university did you attend? Was it a co-ed school? Was it your first choice? Was it hard to get into?

How was your education financed? Did your family pay all or part of your expenses? Did this involve sacrifice? What were your expenses? Tuition? Living? Clothes? Books? Recreation?

If you had a job, what did you do? Did you enjoy it? What was that part of your life like? How much were you paid?

Was your college close enough for you to live at home? Was it a commuting college for most students? Would you have preferred to go away to school?

If you went to an out-of-town college, was this your first time away from home? Can you remember being homesick? Bewildered? How old were you?

Describe your first day on campus. Were you impressed? Overawed? Excited? Confused? What were you wearing? What did you do?

Looking back, do you think you were mature? How did you cope with being on your own?

How did you feel about your studies? Were you a serious student? Had learning come easily to you in high school? Did the new demands and intense competition come as a shock? How did you handle it?

What made you choose your major? Did it hold your interest till graduation? Did you change majors? How often?

Did you feel sufficiently challenged? Were you learning what you had *hoped* to learn and what you *needed* to learn? Looking back, do you wish you had chosen a different major?

Did you have any famous instructors? Did they live up to their reputations? Who were your favorite instructors? What did you like about them? Did you become friendly with any of them? Did they remain friends after graduation?

What college activities did you participate in? Studio art? Choral/instrumental groups? Field trips? Field work? Study abroad? Dramatic productions? College paper or humor magazine? Lab work? College elections?

Do you remember finals week? Endless cups of coffee? Uppers? Cramming? How washed-out everyone looked? Pushing through a crowd to find your final grade?

Was your social life very different from what you had known?

Did you belong to any sororities or fraternities? Which ones? Any stories about Rush Week? Initiations? House Mothers? House Rules? Parties? Guest weekends?

What was the dating situation on your campus? Did you enjoy the social activities? Remember raccoon coats, Model Ts, saddle shoes, bobby socks, sweaters buttoned down the back, going steady, being "pinned"?

How did you feel about college sports? Were you on the team? Were you a cheerleader? Booster? Did you get a Letter? Were you a spectator? Did you date a Letterman? A cheerleader? Tell about the big game.

What did going to college feel like? Were you happy most of the time? Miserable most of the time? Excited about what you were learning and discussing? Excited about your social life? Feeling independent and liking it? Were you scared?

Did you go off with your friends on weekends? Skiing? Camping? Seashore? Did you stay in the dorm and study? Did you have the reputation of being a grind? A play person?

How did college change you? Did it distance you from your family? Your old friends? Were you ever able to bridge the distance? Did you want to? In sum, did you enjoy college?

Did you go to college before the sexual revolution? How did you deal with sexual pressures, your own and from those you dated? What did you and your friends say and think about sex?

Did you go to college *during* the sexual revolution? Did you feel pushed and pulled by the various forces? Were you frightened, angry, elated? How did it affect your behavior? How did it fit into your values? Did it affect your relationships with your family?

Were you post-sexual revolution? Did you benefit from the revolution? Did you lose? Do you think it resolved anything between the sexes? Did sexual freedom release energy for studies?

What did you do in the summers? Travel — where? Work — at what?

Were you in college during a crisis time? Did you take part in strikes, rallies, sit-ins, riots, marches, demonstrations, protest meetings? Did you have confrontations with school authorities? With the law?

Were you involved in politics? What were your political sympathies? Were you part of a radical group? The Vietnam struggle? The Civil Rights Movement? Feminism? Anti-nuclear and environmental activism? A right-wing organization? What influences made you think as you did? Have your beliefs changed? How did it feel to be at the center of that ferment? Looking back, did you make a difference? Would you do it again?

Did you come in contact with the New Wave religious groups? Were your beliefs and religious activities affected?

Did your eating patterns change? What are the differences between the way you ate as an undergraduate and your present diet? The way you dressed and the way you dress now?

Who were your close college friends? How did you meet? What did you do together? What part did they play in your later life?

Was graduation a big moment for you? Describe the ceremony. Was your family there? Your love interest? Did you have a graduation party? Gifts?

Did you know what you were going to do after graduation? Was the freedom frightening? Challenging? Did you end up doing something unexpected? Did your post-graduate experiences live up to your expectations? Did you ever regret going to college?

Do your college years seem different from what you know of college life today? Does the difference seem an improvement? When you see a crowd of college kids, do you wish you were one of them?

Is getting into college harder today? Is it harder to finance? More competitive? Are colleges educating as effectively?

How did going to college affect the rest of your life? If you could, would you do anything differently?

14

Going to Work

Work is what you do to put food on the table and a roof over your head. It might be caviar in a palace but it's still work. A lucky few would work even if they weren't paid for it. Their work is a source of pleasure, challenge, satisfaction, and accomplishment. How was it with you?

What was your first job after you left school? How did you find it? Were you any good at it? How much were you paid? What were your hours?

How old were you when you started to work? What was going on in the world at that time and how did it affect your choice of work or your ability to find a job?

Did you have specific career goals? If not, did you have any ideas about the kind of work you wanted to do? What were they? When and how did you first get them?

What work-related goals did you have when you were starting out?

If you were married, what part did your spouse play in your career choices? Were your parents more or less influential? Anyone else affect your choices?

Did you need to leave home to find work? Where did you go? How did you live? Any interesting job-hunting experiences?

Did you ever belong to a union? Go out on strike? A long one? How did you survive the loss of a paycheck? Did you picket? How did it feel? Did you believe in your union or join because you had to? Was your union a help or a hindrance? How do you feel about unions today?

What was (is) your main work, profession, career? How did you get into it?

What part has your work played in your life? Were you as successful as you had hoped when you started out? Financially? Professionally?

Was your work the most satisfying (least satisfying) part of your life?

Did your work make large demands on your time? Did your spouse contribute to your achievements? How?

Did your work interfere with your marriage? With your relationships with your children? Did you feel guilty? Did you feel forced to the grindstone? Did you use work as an escape? From what?

Tell about a decisive or outstanding moment in your career.

How did you make your own opportunities or take advantage of existing opportunities?

Did you have a mentor, someone who taught or inspired or went to bat for you? Did you choose this person or did he/she choose you? Were there others who helped you along the way? How?

Did you have to pay a price to keep your job? Did you ever feel you were compromised? Given the opportunity, would you be able to handle those problems better now?

What part do you think chance played in your career? What part do you think gender played?

Did you spend most of your life in the same field? Do you have any regrets?

Or did you make a career change? Why? When? What precipitated it? Did the change work for you? Was there more than one important change? Do you believe changing careers was a good idea? Do you recommend it?

Who was the most interesting person you worked with?

Did you inherit a business? As a second or third generation owner how did you compare with your predecessors? Did you feel comfortable stepping into those shoes? Was the family proud of you?

Did you struggle to start your own business? Where did the idea come from? How did you finance it? Did it ever get off the ground? How long did it take? Was it steady growth or were there ups and downs?

What was the greatest business risk you took? How did it turn out? What was your biggest mistake?

Who were your business associates? Did you have a partner? Did you work comfortably together? What kind of employees did you have? Were you on good terms with them? Did you feel they understood your problems? Did you have to deal with a union?

What do you feel is your greatest achievement? What were the greatest strengths you brought to your work? What strengths did you develop in your work?

What are you most proud of about your work history? When you were little could you have imagined having your work experiences? How would you have felt had you known what was ahead of you?

Would you have been equally successful in today's world?

Do you believe the same opportunities exist for young people today?

15

The Single Life

Once upon a time single women were either girls, spinsters, or bad. And single men were either boys, bachelors, or Don Juans. Were you ever afraid you'd end up an old maid? Did you ever wonder if any respectable woman would ever want you? Or did you secretly envy the freedom of "bad" girls and Don Juans?

Did you yearn for a date? Any date?

What was dating like? Did you have a different date every Saturday night? A steady? How did you dress for a date?

What was your dating style? Where did you go? What did you do: Dining? Dancing? Theater? Movies? Picnics? Church suppers? Hiking? Hay rides? Long drives? What was your favorite date? Your least favorite?

Did you and your date keep to yourselves? Did you double date or go out in a crowd? Where did the crowd go? What did the crowd do?

Do you remember the rush of falling in love? Did you fall in love often? Did you hold hands in public? Where did you neck? Front porch? Parlor? In the car? In the great outdoors?

Did you have an unhappy love affair? How did it affect your other activities? How did you get over it? Do you think it left scars? Do you feel warm and nostalgic when you think of it now?

Did you want to get married? Was it your dates who wanted

to get married? How did you try to cope?

Before marriage were you living at home? Did this create problems for you? For the family? Were you able to entertain your friends at home? Did you want to leave home? Would the break have been difficult? How old were you?

Were you focusing more energy on your work when you were single? Were you getting ahead faster?

Did you have more time for your hobbies? Did you have more time for yourself?

Were you sharing an apartment? Were you on a budget? Do you remember apartment hunting? The thrill of having your own place? Fixing it up? Rent time? How old were you then?

How did you get around? Trolley? Subway? Bicycle? Bus? Remember waiting at street corners? Running after a bus? Straphanging? Did you talk to the person next to you?

Did you have your own car? What kind? Was it a gift or did you save for it? How often did it break down? Who fixed it? Any accidents? Remember keeping it clean and shiny? Did you have a name for it? What adventures did you have with it?

Did you enjoy the companionship with your same sex friends? Were you able to continue those relationships after marriage?

All in all did you enjoy the freedom or were you looking forward to "settling down"? Did you have a hope chest? A savings account?

Were you having a hard time finding the right person? What were you looking for? What was your vision of married life? What did you need in order to marry? Money? Job? Promotion? Parents' approval? Freedom from familial responsibility? A divorce?

Was one of your problems that the persons you fell in love with weren't right for marriage and those that were good marriage material you didn't fall in love with?

Were you ever seriously in love before you met your spouse? With whom? What happened?

Did you have more money when you were single? Was your wardrobe better or worse? Were you happier single than married? Were you more your own person when you were single? Did you like yourself more? Less? Do you believe some people were born to be single? Are you one of them?

What was the worst part of being single? What was best about it?

16

Courtship and Marriage

Before the sixties courtship used to lead to marriage and marriage meant a working husband and a housewife. Would you say your relationship took the traditional path? Or did your marriage take place during the maelstrom of change?

How did you meet? Try to relive that moment, those feelings. Was it instant attraction? Did you like the person at all? How old were you? What were your surroundings? What did you talk about? What did you do?

Can you remember the second time you met? How did you and your future spouse get to know each other? Describe your first real date.

Where did you go and what did you do on subsequent dates? Was there one time that was outstanding? What were your favorite things to do together? What about the times that secretly bored you? That made you mad? That made you anxious?

Were there competing love interests in your life at the time? How did you cope with the situation? Did they and this special person ever meet? Come to know about each other? Was there jealousy? What did you do? How did you feel?

Why did you choose as you did?

How long was the courtship? Was it rocky or smooth? What were the greatest difficulties? Did you ever break up? What was the best part of your courtship?

Did you want that particular person, or did you just want guilt-free sex, a convenient mate, the status of being married?

When and how did you decide to marry? Was there a formal proposal? A party? An engagement ring? Was it an heirloom? Did you select it?

What was the family's reaction to your choice of mate? How did your father feel? Your mother? Your siblings? How did your intended feel about *them*? Did you feel torn?

How did you feel about your prospective mate's family? Were you nervous at first meeting? Were their background, interests, and tastes similar to yours? What was the meeting like?

Were you intimate before marriage? How did you feel about that? How do you feel about it now?

How did you manage it? What would have happened if your intimacy were discovered — by your mother? Your father? Your siblings? Your neighbors? Your employer? Were you worried about pregnancy?

Did intimacy draw you closer together? Did it create conflict?

Is this a subject you can talk about with your children? If you can't be open with them about this part of your life, do you think they will be able to be open with you?

How would you feel if you knew *your* parents had been intimate before marriage? Would it have been helpful if your parents had been the kind you could have gone to with your fears and agonies and joys?

When and where did you marry? Was it a big wedding? Formal with a veil, a long gown, and black tie? A religious ceremony? Was it a small wedding? Were you married in a suit? A uniform? Was there a bridesmaid? A best man? Were your parents there? Anyone else?

Did you have the kind of wedding you could afford? Who paid for it? Did you have the wedding you wanted, your mate wanted, or your families wanted?

Describe the reception, wedding breakfast, or supper.

Was the wedding night romantic? Passionate? Disappointing? Funny? Did you have a fight?

Did you have a honeymoon? Where? What did you do? Was it your fantasy of what a honeymoon should be? Did you discover unexpected qualities in your mate?

Did you feel closer to your mate during the first few weeks of your marriage or farther apart?

Any surprises about married life? What were they? Did your mate undergo a personality change after marriage?

What about you? How were you changed by marriage? Did you find yourself enjoying being settled? Hating it? Was constantly having to consider someone else's feelings and opinions difficult? Did you enjoy the sharing?

When was your first quarrel? What happened? Did you wonder if the marriage was a mistake? How was it resolved? Did that quarrel set the pattern for future conflicts?

What was going on in the world during the early days of your marriage? Depression? War? How did this affect your marriage?

In the beginning was yours a traditional marriage with the husband working and the wife keeping house? How did you feel about your new responsibilities? How do you think your spouse felt?

What was the husband's work? How much did he earn? Was it enough for your needs? Did he enjoy his job?

Did his work take him away from home for days at a time? Was that a strain on the marriage?

Do you think of those days as a time of struggle? Looking back how do you feel about that period now?

If the wife worked outside the home, what did she do? Did she want to work or was it because of need? How much did she earn?

How important was her job to her? Was she pulled by conflicts of interest? Was there jealousy about her work?

Did the two of you support each other with advice and encouragement?

Did she have outside help in the home? Did the husband help in the home? Was the routine of household clean-up rather fun or did it seem an endless burden?

Who did the cooking? Was being a good cook a matter of pride? Were daily meals delicious or more like eating to stay alive?

Did you eat out often? As an affordable luxury? To avoid cooking?

Was food a source of conflict? Did you gain weight after marriage? Did either of you have serious problems with your weight?

Do you remember your budget? If you both worked, did you combine your incomes? How much did you pay for rent, food, clothing? Did you have a recreation allowance? Did you allow for impulse buying? If there was only one income was the other spouse given separate, regular, dependable spending money?

Who managed the money? Who spent the most? Did either of you gamble? Did you have a savings account? Did these issues cause resentment?

In general, who made the decisions in your marriage? Did that change over the years? What were the areas of your responsibility? How many of the big decisions did you make? Was there a power struggle? How did you feel about it then? Now? Looking back, how do you feel about yourself as a leader in your marriage? Would you have liked to do anything differently?

Describe your first apartment or home together. Where was it? How was it furnished? Did you enjoy it? What did you like best about it? What least? Do you still have any of your old furniture or decorations?

What did you do for a big bash? What was your favorite form of entertainment? Picture a big night. A big weekend. A happy scene. A tense scene. A hysterical scene.

Did you live near your family? Did you receive any help from them? Did you help them? Were there regular family get-togethers? Did they strengthen the marriage or cause strife? Could you talk to your family about marital problems? Could you talk to your mate about family problems?

Did you enjoy each other's friends? Did one of you (both of you) have a night out with friends periodically? More than once a week? Separate vacations?

Were you involved in community work? Politics? Were you deeply committed? Do you think you were effective? Which campaigns were you involved in? How about cultural affairs? How much of your time did it take? Did you do it for personal satisfaction or to help your career?

Was your mate a help or hindrance? What about the kids, did they join in the fray or were they an obstacle you worked around?

Who outside the marriage was most helpful to you in those

years? Who was most fun to be with? Most supportive? Who outside your marriage did your mate most enjoy?

What were your hopes, dreams, plans, goals? Did your mate share them? What did you do about making them come true? How many of them did come true?

Do you remember the fights you had in the first few years of your marriage? What were they about? Were there tears? Shouting? Silence? Leaving the house? How did you make up? Over the years did you learn to fight comfortably? Which of you had the most explosive temper? Was most inclined to sulk? Stayed mad longest? Were your fights a little exciting? Were they a nightmare? Did they resolve anything? Did you feel better or worse afterwards?

What were the three worst crises of your marriage? How did you handle them?

Describe three of the most satisfying events of your marriage.

Did the two of you laugh a lot? Act silly? Have fun? Cry together? Help each other grow?

Did you buy your first home at this time of your life? Tell about looking for it. Describe the first home you owned. Or describe why you didn't buy, what influence it had in your life, and how you felt (and feel) about it.

Was there a time in your marriage you'd like to live over? Live it over by describing it in detail.

Think about your relationship. What part of it would you wish for some young couple just getting married? What about it do you hope others won't have to suffer? Is there anything you would like to have done differently? How might that have changed things?

All things considered, do you think yours is (was) a good marriage?

17

For Mothers

Childbearing is probably the most awesome, joyful, frightening, portentous thing that can happen to you. It can be a fulfilling career; it can be a trap. For better or worse life is never the same.

Had this pregnancy been planned? Did it sneak by you? Was it a delightful surprise?

Had you been practicing birth control? Did you or your mate feel guilty about birth control? About having babies? Was religion an issue? What are your opinions about child spacing?

When did you first realize you wanted a child? Did your husband want children? Who was more eager? Would you have missed not having children?

How good was your marriage when you discovered you were pregnant? How did the news affect your marriage? Did your husband make a fuss over you during your pregnancy?

Did you have much morning sickness? Were you active throughout your pregnancy? Did you feel fruitful and loved? Uncomfortable and unattractive? How big did you get? Did your husband enjoy your pregnant body? Were the two of you still lovers?

Did you have any training or exercises to ready you for childbirth? Were there any problems with your pregnancy? Were you frightened? Excited?

Was there a baby shower? Who gave it? Were both spouses

invited? Did it adequately supply your needs? Did you feel that you and the forthcoming birth had been truly celebrated?

Do you feel you were ready to be a mother?

Where was your first child born? Who delivered it? Was it an easy birth? Describe going into the delivery room and as much as you can remember of the birth. Was the father present? Where was he? Did you care? Were both parents present? Was anyone else present? Was the doctor or midwife warm and supportive? Did you have some kind of anesthesia?

When were you first able to hold the baby? How did you feel? Was the baby healthy? Beautiful? Ugly? Were there any special problems? Was it the sex you wanted?

Was the bond with the helpless infant strong and immediate? Was it hesitant and uncertain? Did it develop over time? Were you comfortable with the newborn baby? Were you frightened? Were you nursing or bottle feeding? Did you enjoy holding and feeding the baby? Was this a good time in your life?

How did your husband respond to the baby? To the attention you were giving the baby?

What did you name your child? How did you choose the name? Were there any hard feelings about the name? How does your child feel about the name now?

Was the baby baptized? Circumcised? Blessed? Was there a family celebration? Were grandparents a part of those years? Did they interfere? Were they a help?

How long were you in the hospital? Where were you living when you brought the baby home? Did you rent? What was your financial situation?

Who changed the diapers? Who got up for the nighttime

feedings? Did you have help with the baby or the house after delivery? Who washed the diapers? Did you have a scrubbing board? Washing machine? Diaper service? Disposable diapers? How did you manage? Were you tired all the time? Depressed? Elated? Were you utterly focused on the baby or did you have other interests as well?

In your house, was the infant held, nuzzled, sung to, cuddled, talked to, danced with, bounced? By whom?

Did the baby's crying upset you? Was it a happy baby? A difficult baby? A colicky baby? Was there someone to help you in moments of crisis? Did you feel demanding? Defensive? Truly and adequately supported? By your husband? By your family? By your own body?

Was it hard for you to leave the baby with a sitter to go out in the evenings? Did you? Who was the sitter? Was leaving the baby a source of dissension between you and your spouse?

Did you ever leave your baby for a long stretch of time? How long? Why? How did you feel about it? Who took care of the baby? How did the baby react to you when you returned? How did you feel when you returned?

Were you the same age as most new mothers? Did you feel you had lost your young womanhood by being tied down to a baby so soon?

Were you embarrassed at being older than the other mothers? Did you miss out on the camaraderie of sharing child care with your age mates? Were you ever mistaken for your child's grandmother?

Looking back what were the pluses and minuses of having your child at that age?

Did you have a second child? After how long an interval? Were you ready? Did the second child create financial hardships? Time and energy hardships?

How was it different this time? Easier? How did the first child react? What did you name this child? Was there as much excitement as over the first? Did you find yourself secretly liking one more than the other? What about your husband?

Did you find yourself acting as buffer between the children and your husband? Between the children?

What happened when you were tired and resentful and angry at your children? Did your husband help? Was one of your children more responsive than the others? More difficult?

How many children did you have? Over how long a period? Write a little description of each child including birthday, color of hair and eyes, body type, personality, outstanding qualities, special talents, and problems. How were your children alike? How different?

What kinds of things did you do with the children when they were little? Read to them? Roughhouse? Tell them stories? Listen to them? Take them to the museum? The park? The zoo? Ball games? Did you have fun with your children at this age?

What did you and other young mothers do together while you watched the kids? Did you share babysitting? Did you have any time away from your children? What did you do?

What kinds of things did the family do together? Describe a few memorable outings.

Did the children go to nursery school? Do you remember your children's first day at school? Did they cry? Did you feel like crying? Do you think nursery school (preschool, kindergarten) was good for your children? Were there differences in the effects early schooling had on them?

Describe some special moments during their elementary school days. Did they learn much? Did they enjoy their teachers? The other children? Were you aware of any problems? Which of their problems became problems for you? Were you worried about the outside world's influence on them?

Did you belong to the PTA? Were you a den mother? A 4H leader? A Sunday School teacher?

Were you the one responsible for the family's religious participation? Did you meet with much resistance? From whom? Did you make sacrifices for your children's religious training? Were you happy about your children's religious training? Do you feel your religion helped you with your children? Are they still involved with their religion? Have they become involved with a new faith? Do they have a religious life?

Did you make birthday parties and other special treats for your children? Did you have as much fun as they did?

Was your house always full of other people's kids? Did your children appreciate the atmosphere you created? Did you referee slumber parties? Outings? Did you break up pillow fights? Water pistol fights? Fist fights? How about the back seat of the car on a hot summer day?

Were there any scary times with sick children? Did they have to go to the hospital? Did they need surgery? How did they react to the doctors? To the hospital scene? How did you react? Was your husband helpful during medical crises?

Can you describe the first time you realized your kids were no longer looking to you as the ultimate role model? Did you have friends in the same boat?

Many women say they need to have a baby in their arms. How about you? How did you feel when you realized you probably couldn't have another child?

Were you proud of your kids during their adolescence? What were their greatest strengths? Greatest weaknesses? What troubled you most?

Was there tension between you and your teenagers? Did you yell at each other? Were you able to talk to each other? Could you count on their obedience? Were there problems over hair, clothes, sex, alcohol, drugs?

What about alignments in your family? Who sided with your husband? Who sided with you? Did the kids maintain a united front? How heated did it get? Did the sides ever switch? Is the alignment still in effect?

How did you deal with your fears about their driving, drag racing, surfing, skiing, skateboarding, motorcycling . . .? Was your mate helpful? Did he encourage them to be reckless?

How did you feel when they started dating? Did you miss having them around the house? What did you think of their choices?

What was it like to be a mother during the sexual revolution? During wartime? The Civil Rights movement? How did these social crises affect your relationship with your children?

Was there conflict between you and your husband about disciplining your children during their teen years? Did it strain the marriage? Were you able to present a united front?

Do you feel you ever betrayed your kids to placate your husband? Did it estrange your children? Were you able to mend the damage?

Did you have a brother, sister, friend you could share these worries with?

In the face of these problems, what did you do right? Remember gab sessions with your kids, shopping with your daughters, your son's first suit, cheering when your kid scored a point, their first jobs, high school proms?

What are you proudest of as a mother? Would you do it all over again?

MOTHERHOOD AS A CAREER

Did you work before marriage? Before delivery? Were you and your husband in agreement about your staying home? Did you miss your job? Feel less (more) important as a housewife?

Did you stay home with your children by choice or because it was expected of you? Was it fun?

Were you bored and stifled at home? Did you long for adult conversation? Did you feel excited and important at being the hub of your family and the creative center of life?

Who was the *real* boss of your family? Was this openly acknowledged? Did you have limited authority? Were you content to have your husband assume responsibility for the family? Did he do a good job?

Do you think your children benefited from having your full attention? Were they more self-confident? Law-abiding? Loving? Family oriented?

Looking back, do you think your kids were less independent, less resourceful, more demanding than if you'd had a part- or full-time job?

Did you develop hobbies, interests, talents during your children's growing years? Did you participate in afternoon women's clubs? Community activities? Church activities? Did you want to but have no time?

When the children left home, how did you feel: Free? Less burdened? Lost? Left behind? Lonely? Ready to explore a new chapter of your life?

The demands of the mother's role have changed in our time. How do you feel about this? Are you glad you had your babies when you did? How do you think you would feel as a young mother today?

What was life like during your child-rearing years? What was going on in the world? Did you worry about your children's future?

How did you view your role as parent? Do you think you were a good one? How did you feel then? What would you do differently if you could?

Do you feel your spouse was a good parent? In what ways? How did you feel at the time?

What did you learn from child rearing that you would like young mothers to know?

What did you enjoy least about those years? What did you enjoy most?

Did your children have children their own age to play with? Did you enjoy their play? What about the mess and the noise?

THE WORKING MOTHER

What made you decide to be a working mother? Had you worked before the birth of your children? Was your job held for you? Did your career lose momentum due to pregnancy and childbirth?

How old was your child when you began working? How did you decide when was the right time? Did money problems decide for you? Had you fully recovered your strength? Were you still nursing? Were you able to continue nursing?

Did you still have to get up for nighttime feedings? Did your husband take one of the night watches?

How much help was your husband with child care? What did he do that you most appreciated? What didn't he do that you most resented?

Were you able to use some of your income to hire help? Nanny? Babysitter? Housekeeper? Day worker? Did the family help with child or house care?

Describe a typical day.

How did things change when your children went to school?

Did family responsibilities prevent you from accomplishing as much on the job as you wanted? Did you go as far in your career as you might have without those responsibilities? Did this frustrate you?

Did you enjoy working? Would you have quit if you hadn't felt the family needed the extra income?

How did you make time to be with your husband and children? Was there any time left over for you? What did you do with it?

Did working prevent you from being the kind of parent you would have liked to be? Were you tired all the time? Did you feel guilty about not having enough time for the children?

Did the demands on your time and energy interfere with your marriage? Was your affection for your husband eroded by daily resentment about being overworked?

Did the extra money improve family life? Vacations? A home of your own? The kids' education? Business opportunities for your husband?

Did you and your husband pull more closely together in caring for the family? Were you able to build a sense of camaraderie in your sharing of responsibility and chores? Could you retain a sense of humor and fun in spite of the pressure?

How were you affected by the children going off on their own? Did you continue to work? Were you grateful for the work? Were you more effective? Did your job become a more important part of your life?

Do you feel your children were more independent and responsible because you worked? Did they resent your job? Were they proud of you? Do you think your example of discipline and organization infected your children?

Did your daughters follow your example and become working mothers? What comments do your children make about their working mother today?

Do you think a combination of job and motherhood is right for most women?

THE SINGLE MOTHER

How did you survive?

What happened to put you in this situation? With all its difficulties was it easier than when he was around?

Were you able to find work? What was your salary? Did it cover your expenses? Were there opportunities for a better paying job?

What kind of living conditions were you able to provide for yourself and the kids? Could you afford a car? Were medical expenses a problem? How about clothes? Food?

Did you have help from the children's father? Was child support an ongoing struggle? Did the law assist you in obtaining child support?

Did your family help financially? When you were in a jam, did they offer or did you have to ask?

What about help from community services like Aid to Dependent Children? Medicaid? Welfare? Food stamps? Did your religious affiliation provide assistance?

Was there a custody issue? Did you have full custody? Did he have visitation rights? Were you worried about the kids' safety when they were with him? For a time did you mold your private life to conform with what you felt were the court's requirements? Did you ever consider giving your children to your husband's care? Giving them out for foster care? Did you have to do it for a time?

Despite the hardships and rough times were you and the kids able to band together into a close loving unit?

How did you manage your time and energy? When you were working, what about the kids? Who kept the house clean? Who did the cooking? What happened when you were sick?

Did their father find time to be with the children? Did he spoil them? Give them things you couldn't afford? Countermand your decisions, undermine your authority? Were you grateful for some time to yourself? Did you feel defensive about ambivalent feelings? Or were you and their father able to maintain effective teamwork in raising the children?

What did you do about birthdays and holidays?

Did the children want to be with their father? For how long? How did they act after they had been with him? What did they say about it? What did you say and how did you feel?

How did you handle your children's sense of loss? Did they let you know they envied kids who had fathers? Did your children have special problems at school and in the world? Did you worry about a father figure for your kids? Were you ever jealous and resentful of their affection for their father?

Did you feel it wasn't fair: you were the one doing most of the work of caring for them and he was their hero?

What did being a single mother do to your personal life? Did you have time and energy for dating? Money to buy clothes? Did the children diminish your chances with men? Did you bring the men you dated home to meet the children? Were they jealous of your men friends? How did they behave around them? Were they threatened and resentful when you went out on a date? What did you do for privacy? Was your enjoyment shadowed by feelings of guilt?

Did having children make you eager for a second marriage? Did the kids try to push you at men? Did you let them? How did you feel about your children having to deal with a stepfather?

Were there ever moments when you looked at the kids and wished they weren't there? Did you especially miss having a mate when the kids were sick? When you had to discipline? Did you worry about losing control?

What's the hardest part of doing it alone?

Do you and your adult children have a special closeness because of what you went through together? Were there moments when you felt exultant pride at managing on your own?

What advice do you have for a woman suddenly confronted with being a single parent?

18

For Fathers

In the old days men's roles didn't leave much room for active parenting, but there are always exceptions. Perhaps you are one of them. Or do you envy the young fathers of today who participate in every phase of childrearing?

What were your feelings when you first heard your wife was pregnant?

Had you thought about fatherhood before? Had you dreamed about having children? Did carrying on the family line mean anything to you? Did you feel you were ready for fatherhood? Do you think so now?

Had you been practicing birth control? Who had the responsibility for preventing births? Did your wife and you see eye to eye about having children? Did you or your mate feel guilty about birth control? Was religion an issue? What are your opinions about child spacing?

Were you afraid children would limit your freedom? Did you have any fears about what they it might do to your marriage? Did you expect the baby to strengthen your marriage? What was your relationship with your wife like before the pregnancy?

How were your finances at the time? Did you have a good job? Were you prepared for the extra expenses? Did you have to ask for help? Who did you go to?

What hardships did your wife's pregnancies create for you? Was your wife a nuisance during that time?

How did you feel about her body as the pregnancy progressed? Were the two of you still lovers?

Was there any concern over losing the baby? What about the prospect of delivery, was it frightening? To you? To your wife?

Was this the time you began getting in debt? Began distancing from your wife?

Did you feel closer and more protective than ever?

Were you the same age as most first-time fathers? Did you feel tied down too soon? Did you feel foolish about fathering a child late in life? Did your age influence your relationship with your children? Looking back what were the pluses and minuses of fathering a child at that age?

Did you have any part in the delivery? Did you want to? Was the waiting long? Were you alone or with friends? Did you get drunk?

After the child was born did you pass out cigars? Did you feel proud? Awed by this new responsibility? Can you remember the first time you saw your baby? Held it? The first time it gripped your finger? How did you feel? Was the baby healthy? Beautiful? Ugly? Were there any special problems? Was it the sex you wanted?

What did you name your child? How did you choose the name? Were there any hard feelings about the name? How does your child feel about the name now?

Was the baby baptized? Circumcised? Blessed? Was there a family celebration? Were grandparents a part of those years? Did they interfere? Were they a help?

How long was your wife in the hospital? How did you finance the bills? How did you manage on your own? Where were you living when you brought the baby home? Did you rent?

Was the bond with the helpless infant strong and immediate?
Was it hesitant and uncertain? Did it develop over time?
Were you comfortable with the newborn baby? Were you
frightened? Did you enjoy holding and feeding the baby? Did
you help with diapers? The bath? Soothing the baby's cries?
Was this a good time in your life?

Or did you feel your role was to make a living for your family?

How were you earning a living at the time? Were you inspired to work harder? Were you more afraid of failure? Did
the baby interfere with your ability to concentrate and focus
at work?

Was your wife more demanding? Did she give you less attention? Was she giving the baby too much attention? Did she
refuse to leave the baby with others so you could have short
outings? Did she trust you with the baby? Was she critical
about the way you handled the baby? Was this the beginning
of her coming between you and the children?

How often did you find yourself resenting the new baby?
Would your wife or friends have understood? Did you feel
your wife was a good mother?

Did being parents bring you and your wife closer together?

Do you remember the first time your child said "Daddy"? Did
you show off baby pictures? Did you help teach the children
to talk? Walk? Tell them bedtime stories? Hug them a lot?

Did you ever leave your baby for a long stretch of time? How
long? Why? How did you feel about it? Did your wife come
with you? Who took care of the baby? How did the baby react
to you when you returned? How did you feel when you returned?

Did you have a second child? After how long an interval?
Were you ready? Did the second child create financial hard-

ships? Time and energy hardships?

How was it different this time? Easier? How did the first child react? What did you name this child? Was there as much excitement as over the first? Did you find yourself secretly liking one more than the other? What about your wife? Did you find yourself acting as buffer between the children and your wife? Did your wife act as a buffer when the children were getting on your nerves? Was one of them more trying than the others? More worrisome?

How many children did you have? Over how long a period? Write a little description of each child including birthday, color of hair and eyes, body type, personality, outstanding qualities, special talents, and problems. How were your children alike? How different?

What kinds of things did the family do together? Describe a few memorable outings.

Did the children go to nursery school? Do you remember your children's first day at school? Did they cry? Did you feel like crying? Do you think nursery school (preschool, kindergarten) was good for your children? Were there differences in the effects early schooling had on them?

Describe some special moments during their elementary school days. Did they learn much? Did they enjoy their teachers? The other children? Were you aware of any problems? Which of their problems became problems for you? Were you worried about the outside world's influence on them?

Did you belong to the PTA? Were you a scout leader? A 4H leader? A Sunday School teacher?

Who was responsible for the family's religious participation? Was there much resistance from the rest of the family? From whom? Did you make sacrifices for your children's religious training? Were you happy about your children's religious training? Do you feel your religion helped you with your children? Are they still involved with their religion? Have they become involved with a new faith? Do they have a religious life?

As the children grew older did you roughhouse with them? (Did your wife get mad?) What games did you play together? Did you teach them to ride bikes? Fly kites? Build models? Did you fix scraped knees, dolls, dropped ice cream cones, lost baseball games, irate mothers? Did you read to them? Take them to the movies? To the theater? To exhibits? Out camping? Fishing?

Did you enjoy their childhood?

Was your house always full of other people's kids? Did your children appreciate the atmosphere you created? Did you referee slumber parties? Outings? Did you break up pillow fights? Water pistol fights? Fist fights? How about the back seat of the car on a hot summer day?

Were there any scary times with sick children? Did they have to go to the hospital? Did they need surgery? How did they react to the doctors? To the hospital scene? How did you react? Was your wife helpful during medical crises?

Can you describe the first time you realized your kids were no longer looking to you as the ultimate role model? Did you have friends in the same boat?

Many women say they need to have a baby in their arms. Was your wife like that? Did you have a child or two you didn't really want or feel you could afford just to satisfy that need? How did you feel when you realized your wife probably couldn't have another child?

When your kids became teenagers were you able to keep the connection? What interfered? How did you try to bridge the barrier? Did you hear yourself yelling a lot? Did they yell back? How did it feel to find yourself losing authority? With which was it worse, your son or your daughter? Or was there one child who had been especially close who turned away during these years?

When you looked at a teenage son, did you sometimes see yourself at that age? When you looked at a teenage daughter, did you sometimes see her mother? Was their youth and vitality beautiful to you? Did it sometimes drive you crazy?

Were you and your wife arguing about the kids more than when they were little? What were the issues?

What about alignments in your family? Who sided with Mother? Who sided with you? How heated did it get? Did the sides ever switch? Is the alignment still in effect?

What were your fears for them? Drugs? Alcohol? Sports? Drag racing? Hang gliding? Motorcycles? Did you give them permission anyway? Was your wife panicky about these activities? Who won?

What happened when they started dating? Did you lose control of the phone? What did you think of the boys your daughter brought home? Did you ever get to see your son's choices?

What was it like to be a father during the sexual revolution? Wartime? The Civil Rights Movement? How did these crises affect your relationship with your children?

Was your marriage strained during your children's teen years? Did you and your wife manage to maintain a united front?

Do you feel you ever betrayed your kids to placate your wife? Did it estrange your children? Were you ever able to mend the damage?

Could you share these worries with anyone?

In the face of these problems, what did you do right? Remember shared confidences with your kids, fishing, camping trips, taking a picture of your daughter in her prom gown, cheering when your kid scored a point, being in the audience while your kid was performing, their first jobs?

What are you proudest of as a father?

THE SINGLE FATHER

What happened? Why did you have to go it alone? Was it death or separation? Did your grief and anger interfere for a time with your ability to cope? Were the children a comfort? An additional burden?

How old were the kids when you took over? How old were you? Were you freelancing or did you have to go to a job? Did taking care of the children interfere with your work? Your advancement?

What about child care? What were your needs? A housekeeper? Baby sitter? Preschool? What did that do to your salary? Were you paying spousal support as well? Did your standard of living shrink?

What happened when you were sick? Did your family help? Were you doing it all yourself? Did the thought of giving the children up for foster care ever cross your mind? Did you have to for a while?

How did you fare as chief cook and bottle washer? Was it overwhelming or were you proud of your new skills? Were you able to get the kids' cooperation with the family chores? How did you handle the routine?

Describe a typical day.

Did you find yourself badmouthing their mother to the kids? Or defending her to them? How did *that* make you feel?

How much time did the children spend with their mother? Did she spoil them? Countermand your decisions? Undermine or support your authority? Or were you and she able to maintain effective teamwork in raising the children?

Did they want to be with her? How did they feel about their mother? Did they play you against each other? What did they say about her? How did you respond and how did that make you feel?

How did you handle your children's sense of loss? Did they envy kids who had live-in mothers? Did your children have special problems at school and in the world? Was there someone who acted as a mother figure for them? Did they accept her?

What part did grandparents play in your lives?

What about PTA, scouting, church activities? Were you able to spend as much time with the children as you'd have liked? Do you think you would have been able to do a better job as a father if the kids had a live-in mother?

Do you think they were better off with you than they would have been with their mother?

Would you have preferred that their mother raise them? Were there ever moments that you looked at the kids and wished they weren't there?

Did you especially miss having a mate when the kids were sick? When you had to discipline? When your daughter began approaching puberty?

What did being a father do to your personal life? Did you have time for dating? Did the children diminish your chances with women?

Did you bring the women you dated home to meet the children? What happened? Were they jealous of your women friends? How did they behave? Were they hostile and resentful when you went out on a date? Or were they trying to hustle you into marriage?

Did the children's attitudes shape your thinking about another marriage?

What's the hardest part of doing it alone? Did you worry about losing control? When occasionally you did lose control, was it so terrible?

Did you and the children finally create an affectionate family unit?

Is there a special closeness between you and your children because of what you went through together? Were there moments when you felt exultant pride at raising them alone?

What advice do you have for a man suddenly confronted with being a single parent?

19

Adoption

Adoption seems such a logical solution for childless couples and children who need parents. And yet so many emotions intervene. There is the desire for the experience of birth and the continuation of the family bloodline. There are your feelings, your mate's feelings, the reactions of both sets of families to contend with. There are the fears of an unknown heredity to deal with, of poor prenatal care, of the effects of previous trauma.

You had the courage and strength to go ahead. What was it like?

How long had you tried to have a biological baby? How did your failures make you feel?

When did you begin thinking about adoption? What was your first reaction?

What were the pressures leading you to decide on adoption?

Was your mate in agreement with you? Who persuaded whom? Eventually did you both fully want to adopt?

How did your family react? Your friends?

When did you begin the process of adopting a child?

Had you anticipated the number of bureaucratic obstacles? Describe what was involved. How did being investigated as a prospective parent make you feel — resentful, anxious, outraged, inadequate?

Was the social worker assigned to your case cooperative and agreeable?

How would you change the adoption system?

Did you consider adopting a "black market" baby?

Did you obtain your baby from private sources? How did you go about it? What were the advantages/disadvantages over the official procedure?

Was adopting a baby more expensive than having a biological baby? Did the expense create a hardship?

Did you meet your baby's biological mother? How did you feel?

For medical reasons would you like to know at least your baby's parents' medical histories?

Do you want no contact or information about the child's biological parents for any reason?

Was holding the baby in your arms for the first time everything you thought it would be?

Were you given enough time to prepare to receive the child or were you notified only a short time before the child arrived?

How long were you kept in anxiety about being allowed to keep the baby? How did you cope with the anxiety?

Or did you adopt an older child? Was it hard to bridge the gulf of suspicion and defensiveness?

Did you miss having a baby to hold in your arms? Or did you rather feel you had been spared a lot of fuss and bother?

Did you have discipline problems? Do you think it would

have been easier with a biological child?

Did you adopt a child from a different ethnic, religious, or racial background than your own? Has the difference created problems for you? For the child? Has your child suffered from being very much a minority in his neighborhood and schools?

Has discrimination been a wedge between you or drawn you closer together?

Have you adopted a "special needs" child? How did this affect your life — your routine, your finances? Are you receiving some community support?

What are its drawbacks? What are its rewards? Would you recommend adopting a special needs child to others? Do you think anyone has the capacity to be a good parent for a special needs child?

Did you have biological children in addition to your adopted child? Before? After? Do you feel a difference?

Does your adopted child fit in as one of the family? Feel like one of the family?

Is there anyone in the family who feels the adopted child is an interloper? Is getting too much of your attention? Is getting more than a fair share of the family's financial resources? How did you handle the problem?

Did you adopt more than one child? The second time around were the paperwork and uncertainty easier?

Did you ever wish you hadn't adopted? Or was that one of your better decisions?

After your adopted children grew up did the family bonds hold? Are you still close? Affectionate? Are you looking forward to being a grandparent?

Have your adopted children ever tried to find their biological parents? How did you feel? Were they successful? Did you meet their biological parents?

Did their presence in your children's lives change your relationship in any way?

Are your adopted children glad they found their biological parents? Are you?

Are you involved with the foster parent program?

How many children have you cared for?

How does the rest of your family respond to your foster children?

Has the community support been adequate?

How would you change the foster care program?

Is losing the children difficult? Does the pain of prospective loss make you hold back in emotional commitment to the foster child?

Do your foster children ever really become part of your family?

How do you deal with the emotional problems foster children bring with them? The social problems? The educational problems?

Do you feel that commonly the teen years are harder for adopted and foster children than for biological children? Are they likely to use their adopted or foster status as an issue around which to crystallize their resentments and fears?

Do your foster children keep in touch with you?

20

Divorce

No matter whether you wanted it or your mate wanted it, divorce is a time of wrenching pain. For some the wounds never heal. This section will help you take a fresh look at that difficult transition.

Had you been happy during the early years of your marriage?

Which of you wanted out? What were the early warning signals? When did you begin to worry? Describe the problem as you saw it then.

Did you separate? Had you wanted the separation to be permanent? Was living apart less painful than living together? Less lonely?

Have you remained separated but not divorced? Does it make you feel less guilty? Is long-term separation an amorphous hell?

Does separation allow you the freedom you want as well as protection from marriage-minded suitors?

Would you love to go all the way and divorce, but can't for religious reasons? Is your faith surviving the pain?

Did the split result in divorce? How old were you at the time? How old were you at the time of the final decree? Had you waited too long to rebuild a satisfactory life?

When you were breaking up, did divorce carry a social stigma? A religious prohibition? Did your family and friends support or condemn you?

IF YOUR MATE LEFT YOU

Was there someone else? Who? An old friend? A work companion? A stranger? Was the interloper much younger? Richer? More attractive? More successful? More carefree? Do you think anyone happening along at this moment could have filled the need?

What did you see as the real reason? Had you grown in different directions? Was your mate running away from failure? Immature? Tired of domesticity? How about denial of age? Was that a factor?

How did you find out that your spouse had a lover? What did you do? Do you ever wish you had reacted differently?

Did you feel your marriage was worth fighting for? How did you fight? When did you realize it was hopeless? How did you react?

During that turmoil, what feelings surfaced most frequently? Fury? Fear? Grief?

What about disbelief: "I love you so much, you MUST love me back." Did you have the feeling it was all a mistake and the difficulties would solve themselves?

At first did you feel it was your fault? That somehow you were lacking? Undesirable? Inadequate? Were you angry at yourself? How did you cope?

Were there times you felt it was all the other person's fault? And wanted to shake some sense into your spouse? Punish? Get even? Did you act on those feelings? What were the consequences? Do you wish you had behaved differently?

Describe your feelings about your mate's lover. And don't

spare the adjectives!

Did you succumb to the temptation to blame this "homewrecker" for the breakup of your marriage?

Was there a period when you escaped from the pain into alcohol, sleeping pills, tranquilizers? Into work? Changing jobs? Leaving the neighborhood, the city, the state?

What about a "rebound" love affair? Did it rebuild your wounded confidence? Relieve your vindictive feelings? Distract attention from your sense of loss? Did it help?

How did you keep your pain from spilling over onto the children? What did you do when you weren't successful? How did the children show their anger at you for the breakup?

When did you start regaining your sense of self? What helped the most? Describe your first successes. Who helped in the process?

Looking back are you proud of having survived? Do you think you're stronger for it? Is your life better now? In what ways?

IF YOU LEFT YOUR MATE

Why did you find it impossible to stay? How did you feel about your spouse at this time? Did you just intend a separation? Did you still have hopes for the marriage? What did you do to try to save it?

Had your mate become violent? Verbally abusive? Unendurably dull? Still a likable person but no longer attractive to you?

At what point did you give up hope of salvaging the relationship?

Did the separation interfere with your job? Require you to

take a job? Did work suddenly become more important? How?

Did you edge into a new lifestyle? Was it more satisfying than the domestic routine?

After the initial confusion and pain, did you have the feeling of finding yourself again? Of feeling lost?

Were you drinking more? What about drugs? Or was that what you were running away from in your mate?

Had you found someone else? Had you been looking? What was it you were looking for? Were you considering divorce or were you just looking for diversion?

Were you taken unawares? What were the qualities that attracted you? Were you still committed to your spouse when you first met?

Were YOU running away from failure? Were you flattered by the attentions of someone new? Did you find conquest stimulating? In those days, were the beginnings of a relationship more rewarding than the stable routine of marriage? Did you find "legal" sex boring?

Did you enjoy showing your lover off to your friends? Or did you hide the relationship? Did hiding make you feel guilty? Anxious? Angry? Did it harm the new relationship?

Did you discover the excitement of an affair was what you had been missing? Was the discovery unsettling? How did you react when your lover began to get serious?

At first, did you blame the affair on your mate's inadequacies? Were you short tempered at home? Impatient with the family? Did your spouse sense something was wrong and try to discuss it with you? How did you respond? How did you feel?

Had you hoped this relationship would not interfere with

your marriage? When you found the affair threatened your marriage, were you angry at your lover? Your family? Yourself?

Did you try to break off the relationship? Because of love and loyalty to your spouse? Reluctance to break up the family? Fear of harming the children? How did you deal with the torment?

Or did you use the affair to get out of a marriage that was already dead? Did you arrange for your spouse to "discover" the affair? Did your spouse resist the discovery? What did you do?

When the affair was acknowledged, what was the reaction at home? Fury? Tears? Threats? Pleading? Icy withdrawal? Appeals to reason? Legal action?

Were the children involved in the battle? Did you feel your relationship with them was threatened?

DIVORCE

What made you realize divorce was inevitable?

In retrospect, what do you think were the real causes of your difficulties? Personality incompatibility? Different values? Different interests? Sexual problems? Money problems? Immaturity? Power struggles?

When had communication broken down? How? Were you throwing words at each other or using silence as a barrier? Did you make efforts to talk about your differences? What was the reaction? Can you think of anything that might have kept you together?

Was the actual breaking up friendly? What arrangements did you make about the children?

Were you or your spouse using the children as pawns? Did you have the panicky feeling you might lose them? Did the possibility of court interference worry you? Or was the court your ally?

Did the children begin to show emotional problems? Did they quickly stabilize? Do they have wounds that haven't healed?

Do you think the two of you were able to reach a fair financial settlement? What does your spouse think? Describe the settlement. How could it have been improved? Did it leave you with a lower standard of living?

Which of you changed residences? Did you have to give up some possessions that were important to you? How did you divide the accumulated mementos of your life together?

Did it become a legal battle? Did the lawyers take over? Are you sorry now you went to court?

Are you sorry you didn't go to court?

Is the memory of the breakup still painful?

Did the divorce estrange you from your traditional faith? Do you feel guilty? Cut off from religious comfort? Cut off from God's mercy? Does your church's position regarding your divorce weaken your authority with the children? Has your church's position regarding your divorce weakened your children's faith in the religion of their birth? Who are you angriest at — yourself, the church, life?

Looking back, do you think you contributed to the problems in your marriage? What could you have done differently?

At this point do you think the divorce was for the best? Are you healthier now? Looking better? Is the new life you created more satisfying?

21

Remarriage

The second time around is a chance to learn from the pitfalls of the first. There is the possibility of realizing lost dreams and the opportunity to build a new life.

Was your first marriage a good one? How long did it last? How did it end? When your spouse was gone, did you feel married life was over for you? How successful were you at living alone?

Or weren't you alone? Were you trying to cope as head of a family? Who did you have to take care of? What was your financial situation? Did you have the opportunity to improve it?

Was money not the problem? Were empty days and lonely nights the enemy? How did you fill them? Did you think of remarriage as a solution?

Did you begin deliberately looking for a mate? In social activities? Singles bars? Travel tours? At work? Did your friends try to help? Did you like the new freedom from responsibility?

How did you feel about sexual intimacy outside of marriage? Were you looking forward to it? Afraid of it? Did religious or moral values prevent you from enjoying sexual intimacy without marriage? Did your standards limit your choice of partners?

Did you welcome the new sexual opportunities? How did you fare in the single world?

What qualities were important to you at this time in your life? Did you have a list?

How did you meet? By your design? Did you stumble on each other? Or did the other person find you?

What got to you first about this new person? How did you feel when you began to realize it was becoming serious? Did you welcome or run away from a new relationship?

What about sex? Were you comfortable about it? Afraid? Had you missed it? Did you feel awakened to be sexually loved again?

What did you enjoy most about being together? What interests did you share? What made you realize this was spouse material?

When did second thoughts begin to appear? What were they? How were they calmed?

At what point did you take each other to meet the families? Describe their reactions. Were you surprised?

What were the obstacles to your marriage? For a time were they insurmountable? Did you solve them? Did they vanish? Or did you ignore them? Are you living with them still?

What kind of wedding did you have? Was it completely private? A big party? Did the family and all the children attend? How did you feel?

Was there a honeymoon? Where? Was it a success? Did it bring you closer together? Reveal new aspects of each other?

What was involved in merging your two separate lives? Did you make a formal pre-nuptial agreement? Did you have an informal understanding of roles and responsibilities? Or were such preliminaries considered calculating and unromantic when you were getting married?

How did you decide where to live? Were there children still living at home? Were you combining families? How did they feel about these new arrangements? Were they pleased to have two parents in the house? Did your new mate truly help with the work and worry of child rearing? Did resentment and a battle of wills spring up? Did it ever ease?

How about grown children? Did they give you a hard time? How did you help them adjust? Are they still resisting?

How did remarriage affect your career? What problems did it create? Was the new spouse an asset?

What about the family income? Was it combined? Who was in charge? Was it the same person who kept the books?

Did you keep your resources separate? Did you share expenses? How did you decide what was fair? Did financial arrangements become an issue in your new relationship?

Do you think this sense of "yours" and "mine" diminished intimacy? Could it have reinforced a feeling of separation between the families? How could that have been prevented?

If you had it to do over, how would you arrange finances?

What did you learn in your first marriage that helped you in your second?

Does remarriage beat being single? Is the second time around better? All in all, would you do it again?

22

Mid-Life Joys and Crises

As the life span increases middle age keeps getting later and later. Someone said, "Life begins at forty." Now youngsters in their sixties start new careers, new marriages, and new families.

How old were you when the children became independent? Was freedom as good as you thought it would be? How did you adjust to their absence? Did it affect your relationship with your spouse? Were you a victim of "Empty Nest Syndrome"?

Why did the kids leave home? College? Work? War? Travel? Marriage? The single life?

Did you like the life they were leading? Did they keep in touch?

Whom did the children marry? What were the pluses and minuses of their mates? Has your opinion changed with time?

Were you still helping the kids financially? What was the money being used for? Education? In business? Was it a struggle? Did you take risks? Use up savings? Mortgage the house? Borrow on insurance? How much did you contribute? Over what period of time? Did they pay it back? All or part?

Did you want to help? Did you feel you had to? Do you think the kids might have been better off if they'd done it on their own? Are you glad you were able to help them? Are they?

Had you reached the peak of your earning capacity and job status at this time? What was your financial situation during these years? Was your work still a challenge? A grind? Were you considering a second career? Looking forward to retirement?

Were you enjoying your new freedom? Did your horizons expand? What about "dreams come true"? Extensive travel? Theater? Concerts? Dining out? In fancy restaurants? Major purchases? An RV? A boat? New car? A house in the country? A condo in the sunbelt?

Did you pour more time and energy into the community? Which project did you enjoy most? What about politics? The arts?

Which activities gave you the most problems? How did you handle bureaucracy, red tape, and difficult characters? Any new friendships? Exciting personalities? Satisfying accomplishments?

What about your sisters and brothers? Were you still close? Were YOU the one keeping the family together?

How was your health? Had your body begun to turn on you? Did you have job-related health problems? Did you begin to take better care of your body? Still smoke? What about alcohol? Exercise regularly? Were your teeth holding up?

Did you take up a new sport? A new hobby? Some adult education courses?

Was there an incident or period during this part of your life that you think of as a mid-life crisis? What was its outcome?

MARRIAGE IN THE MIDDLE YEARS

Had it become cozy and comfortable, with the two of you achieving a new depth of understanding? Had you settled into a mutually satisfying pattern of bickering? Or did you stay together because it felt like there was no place else to go?

Tell about a crisis in your marriage. Does it seem funny now, or are you still afraid it will come around and hit you again?

Describe some warm and tender moments in your marriage.

What was your relationship with your children as they became increasingly independent? How would you like it to be different? What do you and the children like or dislike about each other?

What about grandchildren? How did it feel to become a grandparent? Did that new generation thrill you? Would you just as soon watch them grow from a distance? Do you do a lot of babysitting?

Are you determined to be as wonderful to your grandchildren as your grandparents were to you? Or do you want to give your grandchildren what you missed? Is your relationship with your grandchildren somewhat marred by fear of offending your children? Do you worry about their lack of discipline? About the kind of world they are going to have to live in?

Does watching that new life fill you with joy? And do the grandchildren wear you out after a few hours? What differences did you find between caring for your own children and your grandchildren?

What was your children's relationship with your parents at this time? Did your parents get to know their great-grandchildren?

How did this time of your life compare to your teens and twenties in terms of excitement? In terms of satisfaction? Did you like yourself better?

23

Where Are You Now?

A look at your present life will help you realize that no matter what your age, you still have things to look forward to and choices to make.

What is your age as you write this? How does it feel to be this age?

How do you look? Do you feel comfortable about your appearance? Do you think you are aging gracefully?

How is your health? Any problems? How do you deal with them? Do you worry about your health?

Where do you live and with whom? If you live alone, how do you feel about it? How do you manage the details of daily life?

What is your work? How long do you plan to continue to work? Do you have any specific plans for retirement?

What effect do you think the presence or absence of children had on your life? If this was a deliberate decision, do you think it was the right one for you? In what way?

If your marriage ended with the death or divorce of your spouse, when did this occur? How did you cope with the loss?

Did you remarry or enter other relationships? When? You might want to discuss the differences in your marriages, other relationships, spouses, or partners.

What part did/do friendships play in your life?

How have your values changed over the years? Is there anything that was once important and no longer matters?

Is there anything that became more important as you grew older?

What about your religious beliefs? Have they changed over the years? If so, what caused them to change?

And your political beliefs? Have they changed? In what way? What caused these changes?

Are there other ways in which you have changed (except for your age) or do you feel that inside you are the same person you always were?

Do you think about your future? What do you think of as "old age"? Have you made any plans for yours? What are they?

Are your parents still alive? How are they (and you) dealing with their old age?

Has the death of important people in your life isolated you or made you aware of your own mortality? Are you afraid of death? What do you do about your fears?

What hobbies and interests that you maintained in your earlier years have paid off now, either in money or pleasure?

Have you thought about or started a new career in this part of your life? Tell about it.

If you have children, where do they live? What is your relationship with them these days?

Do you keep up with old friends? Are you busy making new friends? Which occupies you more now — friends or family? Which is more satisfying?

What was your dream for this part of your life? Can you realistically achieve any part of the dream? Have you already realized the dream?

IF YOU NEVER MARRIED

Do you have any regrets or was this the right path for you?

What are your sources of joy and satisfaction?

What part did love play in your life? Did you have a serious long-term relationship? Are you still in it? If not, what happened?

Who is the most important person in your life now? Why?

What is the most important activity in your life at this time?

If you did not have a primary relationship or a family, do you think you missed something or do you feel relieved when you look at friends who did?

What is your relationship with your brothers or sisters? What part do their families play in your life?

Did you have some adventures (accomplishments) that would have been impossible if you had family ties? What were they?

How do you feel about your career? How did your single status affect it?

Are you still working or are you retired? If you are working, is it by choice or necessity? What is your work? How long do you plan to continue to work?

Do you have any specific plans for retirement?

What do you see yourself doing five years from now? How about in ten years?

24

Retirement

Retirement used to be thought of as being "put out to pasture." The truth is that the current bunch of seniors are active, involved men and women who have become a powerful political, social, and economic force. Many are starting new careers and the remainder are providing the largest pool of volunteers into the nation.

At what age did you retire? Why did you do it? Do you have any regrets about your decision? Is retirement all it's cracked up to be?

How do you feel about mandatory retirement?

What are you doing with your time? Are you busier now than ever?

Are you deeply engaged in community work? Is everyone's attitude, "You can surely take this on now that you've got plenty of time"?

Did retirement mean a new career? How did it get started? How's it going? Is it more fun than your earlier work?

Are you having a difficult time finding a way to channel your passion for life?

Or are you caught in the doldrums and having a difficult time feeling passionate about *anything*? Does this seem to be a period of endurance and watching life slip away from you?

Are you now able to devote as much time to your hobbies as

you'd hoped? Is it paying off in increased satisfaction?

What about friends? Do you have new ones who are part of your new career? Are you able to spend more time with old friends?

What is your financial position? Can you afford to live as you did before retirement? If you have had to reduce expenses, what did you give up?

Have you stayed in the same home? Do you have old friends nearby? Who are they? What kinds of things do you share?

How do you spend the time you previously devoted to your work and/or family?

You probably spend more time with your spouse than ever before. How has this affected your relationship?

Have you relocated since your retirement? Where? Why did you decide to move? Why did you choose this place?

Describe your adjustment to your new community. How long did it take to feel at home? How does your spouse feel about the change? Was it a wise move?

Are your children living close by? Is traveling to visit them one of the joys of retirement? What is your relationship with them these days? How do you feel about it?

If you have grandchildren, how often do you see them? What part do they play in your life now?

What was your dream when you thought of retirement? If you could go anywhere and do anything, what would you do with the rest of your life?

25

Looking Back

Choose a few exciting, challenging, happy, or deeply satisfying times to share with your loved ones.

What period of your life do you think of as the happiest and most fulfilling? Tell about it.

If you could go back and change something, what would it be and how would you change it?

Everyone has stories of missed opportunities. Tell some of yours.

There must also have been opportunities seized and used. How did you recognize and take advantage of them?

What part has luck played in your life? Tell about the luckiest thing that ever happened to you.

Was there an especially difficult time? How did you cope?

Have you had an experience that changed your life? What was it?

Who was the person who had the greatest influence on you? In what way?

What part did love play in your life? How about anger? Fear? Revenge? Hope?

Was there a dangerous habit that got hold of you? Drinking? Drugs? Gambling? Risking life and limb? How did you get into it? Have you stopped? How? What did it give you? What did it take away? How would you feel if some young person you loved started doing the same thing?

Did music play an important part in your life? When were you first aware of it? What kind of music meant the most to you? Try to explain the kind of pleasure music gives you and its place in your life. Who were your favorite artists? Have your tastes changed over the years? Did you go to live concerts? Collect recordings? Listen to the radio? Was this something you did with friends or by yourself? Did you pinch pennies in other places to indulge your love of music?

What about the arts? What medium is your favorite? Are you a collector? Do you haunt exhibits? Which affected you the most strongly? Is there one artist who is especially important to you? A particular style? Have your tastes changed over the years? Describe as best you can the kind of pleasure art gives you. Which do you think affects you most strongly, color or design?

Are you a reader? Fiction or nonfiction? Poetry? Who are your favorite authors? Do you go to books for escape or information? For vicarious adventure? Intellectual stimulation? For the sensual beauty of language? When did you start reading avidly? Has your taste in books changed over the years? Do you use the library or buy books? Do you have a storage problem? Have you ever had to move your library?

Have foods always meant a great deal to you? Describe one of your most memorable feasts. A great glut. A junk food binge. A trip that was memorable for its food. What style of cooking do you most enjoy? Has your taste changed with time? Do you cook? List some of your all-time favorite restaurants.

What about sports? Do you prefer going to the game or watching on TV? Which is *your* game? What do you like most about it? Who is your all-time favorite player? Do you bet on the games? What was your most satisfactory win? What do you like most, the sociability that goes with sports or the game itself? Can you describe the pleasure watching sports gives you? Who in your family shares your enjoyment?

Who were some of the most memorable people in your life? The most nurturing? The funniest? The most interesting? The most difficult? The most companionable? The most honest? The biggest rascal? The most lovable? How did you meet? What part in your life did they play?

What do you consider the most important events in your personal life? Tell about them.

Have you ever had any unusual spiritual, religious, or mystical experiences? How did they affect you?

If you could stop the clock at any age, when would that be? Why then?

26

The Family History

The following studies go beyond your personal history into the story of your family. These questions will help organize your recollections and information. If you want to do a serious genealogical study, you will find recommended books and publications in the section on Researching Your Roots.

Was family pride a tradition in your home, or were you the first to begin searching for your roots?

What's the first mention of your family name that you could find? Where did you locate it? Does it have a meaning? What is its history?

Who were your earliest known ancestors? Where did they live? (Country, town, etc.) Were any of them famous? Infamous? Were they explorers, pioneers, sailors, peddlers, pirates, musicians, statesmen, tailors, farmers, artists? How did they make their living?

Do their skills or talents reach down through the generations into present times?

Were any of your ancestors Native Americans? How much of their history survives?

Unless you're a Native American, there are immigrants in your background. Who were they? When did they emigrate? Why did they leave the Old World? Did war, hunger, persecution, politics play a part in their lives? How?

How did they travel? Where did they settle? What difficulties and hardships did they encounter and how did they meet these challenges?

What was their ethnic and religious background? Does your family still carry on that tradition?

What do you know about their social and economic position? What incidents reveal or demonstrate this? Do you have any stories about their personal lives? Love stories? Tales of courage? Funny stories? Tragedies?

Who were the dominant figures in the family? What areas of family life did men control? Where was the women's power?

Did men and women have different dreams, achievements, frustrations?

Were there any famous members of your family? Infamous ones?

What about your ethnic group of origin do you most prize? Do you find any of those characteristics in yourself?

Do you have an ancestor you are particularly proud of?

Do you own any furniture, china, art, diaries, or other mementos from an ancestor? What is it? How did it come to you?

There may be some family legends you'd like to pass on. How did you happen to hear them?

27

Your Grandparents

Grandparents are special for those who were lucky enough to have known theirs. They were a source of love and understanding. Through them we glimpsed distant generations and felt the link to bygone days.

Close your eyes and try to remember your grandparents when you were a child. How did they look? Were they tall, short, plump, thin? Did they wear glasses? Picture them, hear their voices. Write about the image that appears in your mind.

What did you call them when you were little? When you were an adult? What were their formal names?

Do you have any special memories of their home? Describe it, the place, furniture, colors, sounds, smells. Try to recall an incident that took place in that setting.

Where did they live? Do you remember the neighborhood? The climate?

What kind of personalities did your grandparents have? Were they serious, grim, funny, happy, hardworking? Did they tell you stories? How did they react to each other? To your parents? To you?

What did you like most about them? What annoyed you?

Can you remember family celebrations, gatherings, holidays in which your grandparents participated?

Were there any special private moments with a grandparent?

Did one of them play an important role in your life? This
could be a rich source of material to give to your own children and grandchildren.

What do you know about the kind of lives your grandparents
had? Where were they born? Have you learned anything
about the saga of their lives?

What was their world like? Their neighborhood?

How long did they live? Did they have a good old age?

*If you never knew your grandparents you may have been told
about them by your own parents or by other relatives.* If so,
who told you? What do you think the teller was feeling? How
did that make you feel?

When and where did you hear these stories? How old were
you?

How do you feel about never having known your grandparents? Are you trying to give *your* grandchildren the relationship you never had?

Was there someone in your life who functioned as a grandparent? In what ways? When? What do you know about his
(her) history?

What stories or legends have been handed down about your
grandparents?

Do you own anything that belonged to your grandparent?
What is it? What does it mean to you?

28

Your Parents

If your parents are alive you might be able to use the questions to interview them. They'd probably love the chance to share their recollections. Taping your interviews will give a permanent record. You might want to videotape some of the sessions.

Unfortunately, many of us no longer have living parents. Memories are filled with emotions, some painful, some happy. Just tell your stories as you remember them.

Of course, most of these questions apply to both parents. However, it's best to think of each parent separately. When you finish making notes about your memories of your mother, go back over the same questions with your father in mind. Any time a question triggers a memory that doesn't belong to the story you're writing, make adequate notes and save it for future use.

WHEN YOUR PARENTS WERE YOUNG

Where and when were they born? Was money a problem for the family? Where did their money come from? Were they cared for by a nursemaid? Did your parents have many advantages as they were growing up?

Did your parents know poverty? Did they have to work when they were little? Did you hear stories of their having to do without?

Did your parents travel to other countries when they were little? Why? What stories did they tell you about their journeys?

What was their ethnic and/or religious background? Was any language besides English spoken in their home? Did they pass it on to you? Did your parents speak English with an accent? How did you feel about it?

What were their stories about coming to this country? About the old country? Did they miss it?

How did their background affect the way they were brought up? Did its influence on them affect your life?

What do you know about your parents' education? Was school different in their day? Were they self-educated? How much schooling did they have? Did they use their education in their adult life?

Did they want the same amount or more education for you? Did they want a different kind of education for you? Were they afraid of your teachers? Impressed by your teachers? Indifferent to them?

What did your parents like most about their childhood? The least?

How many brothers and sisters did they have? How did they get along? Who were your parents' favorite siblings?

Did either of your parents ever reveal their youthful hopes and dreams? As far as you know, which came true? Which didn't?

What was going on in the world when they were young? Did they grow up in wartime? In a depression? In a time of prosperity?

THEIR COURTSHIP AND MARRIAGE

Do you think your parents loved each other? How did they act together? Did you ever see them holding hands? Being even more intimate? Did they tease each other?

Did either of them ever tell you stories of their courtship? How did they meet? How long did they go together before they were married?

When and where were they married? Did the world feel like a safe place then? Were their families happy about their marriage?

What kind of wedding did they have? Did they have a honeymoon?

How long before they had their first child? How many did they have? What do you know about their lives before you were born?

Can you remember them as young parents? Where did they live? What were they like? How did they act with each other? Did they share interests? Tastes? Ideals? Political views?

How did your father earn a living? Was the family well to do? Poor? Did your mother have a job outside the house?

Did anyone besides your mother take care of you? How did you feel about that person? Were you ever spanked? Cuddled?

Did your mother and father argue about how to raise the children? Did they argue about money? Other things? Did they laugh a lot? Did they have parties?

Was your father ever out of work? How did it affect him? Did he become silent and reclusive? Do you think he was ashamed? Did he shout a lot? Do you think he was angry?

Did they have to cope with being poor? Did your parents buy food on credit? With food stamps? Was there enough food? Could your mother make a delicious meal out of nothing?

Did your mother sew her own clothes? Were you ever embarrassed about the way your parents dressed?

How did you feel about your home? Did you think it was ugly? Attractive? Comfortable? Were you able to invite friends or was this a problem for you? How did your parents treat your friends?

Maybe your family was well to do. Were you aware of people who had more than you? Less than you? How did you feel about them? How did you feel about yourself?

Were your parents religious? Was one more religious than the other? Do you think their religion nourished them?

Was your mother beautiful? Plain? What about her voice? The way she moved? Did you enjoy looking at her? Listening to her? Being around her?

How did you see your father?

How did your mother enjoy being a wife? Do you think she was more lover, housewife, or mother?

Was your father a real family man? Did he and your mother work and play together? Who was the boss? Was it a happy arrangement?

Imagine an important day in your parents' lives. Describe it as if your mother were telling you about it.

Now tell the story as your father would have told it.

Was either of your parents ever seriously ill? What was the problem? How did it affect the family?

Did their relationship change during the years? How did your emerging adulthood affect them?

Did your parents ever separate? Did they get a divorce? What did they tell you about it? What did you believe? How did it affect your family life? Did your mother have to go to work?

Did you wish your parents would divorce? Did you feel home was a battlefield?

Did your parents remarry? Were the new marriages good ones? Were they different kinds of marriages? Did they make your parents happier? More secure?

What effect did this have on your life? Did your parents' marital problems make you suspicious of marriage and commitment?

If you had a step-parent, what part did he/she play in your life? If you had a close relationship with a step-parent you might choose to refer to the questions about natural parents.

Did either of your parents remain single after divorce? Which one? By choice? Was he/she lonely? Bitter? How did this affect you?

If they had a long life together, did they become more intimate or draw away from each other as they grew older? Did they quarrel more? Did they still hold hands?

You must have thought about your parents' relationship. How did it appear to you when you were a child? Do you perceive it differently now?

Did you ever feel they were a closed unit you couldn't become part of? Did you ever feel like a referee? Torn between them?

How do you think your parents would feel about the changing roles of men and women today?

In what ways did your leaving home affect your parents? Did they help you to get established?

Did your parents live to see grandchildren? What did they think of *you* as a parent?

Did they come to live with you in their old age? Near you? How did that work out?

Did they move into a retirement home? A convalescent home? Were they comfortable? Did they want to live with you? Did you feel they *should* be living with you? Did you feel defensive and angry? Did you worry about them?

Are they still alive? What is old age like for them? Are they afraid of losing each other? Of dying?

Have you already lost your parents? To an accident? A catastrophe? An illness? Were you able to help care for them? Did helping sap your resources? Did your spouse resent it? Your children? Did you resent it?

Did the final illness change their personalities? How?

Where did they die? Was it a "good" death?

What about your parents made you feel the most proud? Least proud? What did you like the most? The least? What made you the angriest? What was the most lovable?

These days do you often remind yourself of your parents? When? In what way? How do you feel about it?

29

Interviewing Sisters and Brothers

Brothers and sisters, if you have them, have seen your life from a different perspective. Their views can be fascinating. You'll be surprised how often your memories will differ. Their memories, even when they run counter to your own, often open up forgotten avenues.

Interviewing them will be a valuable resource for your project. You can do it by mail, by phone, or in person. You can tape them or videotape them. A combination of techniques may be the most satisfactory: a personal interview with the warmer nostalgic questions that will evoke laughter and teasing, while you save the hotter, more volatile questions to be asked at a safe distance by mail.

However you approach the interview, it will enrich your stories and it may heal old wounds and draw the two of you closer together.

Most of the questions relating to your family of origin will serve you well in interviewing your siblings. The following questions are especially designed to evoke their memories of you and your effect on their lives.

Where was the first place you remember?

When you were little what did Mom and Dad look like? What were Mom and Dad like before I was born? Do you think they were enjoying life? Was their relationship better or worse after I was born?

How did they treat you when you were little? When you were a teenager?

Do you remember whether Mother was happy about being

pregnant with me? Did they tell you about it beforehand? When was the first time you saw me?

Did my birth change anything for you? What was the worst part of having a baby (an older) sibling? The best part?

Were you less lonely after I was born? Did you have more chores? Did you have less attention from Mother? From Father?

Did we have clothes problems? A room problem? Did we ever share a bed? Did we have water fights in the bathtub? Did Mother ever let us be alone in the bathroom together?

Can you remember family meals when I was little? What did we eat? What were your favorite foods? Do you remember my favorites? Did we gang up together with our food preferences?

What is your memory of the family finances in those early years? Did we have a car? What kind was it? Where did you sit in the car? Or did we use public transportation? Can you remember what it was like?

Did Mother have a washing machine? A washboard? Diaper service? Did she have help? Were you her help?

Did you have to babysit me? How did you feel about it? How did I do as a babysitter? What were other babysitters like? Did we like them?

When the folks put you in charge, did I mind you? Was I easy to take care of?

Was I mean to you when the folks left us alone? Were you ever afraid of me? Why?

Later on did you have to take me with you when you went out playing with your friends? Did you try to get out of it? How? What did I do on those outings?

Did we ever fight? Verbally? Throw things? Hit each other?

Who were Mom and Dad's favorite relatives? How did you feel about them? What about their friends? Do you remember them playing or talking to us?

What did I do that made you the angriest as a small child? As a teenager?

Which of us do you think had the easier time at school?

Among us children who do you think was Mother's favorite? Dad's favorite? Did you feel there was enough love to go around in our house? Which could you talk to most openly? Which was the most fun to be around?

Do you think of yourself more as Dad's child or as Mother's child? Do you think they knew how you felt? Do you think our parents treated us equally? Do you think I had an easier time of it than you did? Why?

Did you feel protective toward me when I was little? How did you feel when I was being punished?

Did you feel safer when I was around? Could you count on me to be on your side when you were in trouble? If the folks were angry with you? Did you feel you could talk to me?

Did you feel I took sides against you with Mother, with Father, with the other kids?

What did we do together that you especially liked? What was the nicest thing I ever did for you? The meanest?

What was my most annoying habit? What did I do that secretly tickled you? That you were envious of?

What could have been done to make our relationship better when we were little? When we were teenagers?

How did you feel about my boyfriends? My girlfriends? Did you ever feel left out? Did we drive you crazy? Were you worried about the kind of people I associated with? Could you talk to me?

Did I have a temper when I was little? Was I stubborn? Frightened? Shy? Sassy? How about when I was a teenager?

Do you see us in your own kids as they are growing up? Do they get along better than we did? Worse? What do you think made the difference?

How did you feel the first time you knew I had been intimate with the opposite sex? Did it make a difference in our relationship?

How did you feel when I got married? When I had my first child?

Do you hope your children will have the same kind of relationship with each other as we did?

How has our relationship changed over the years?

Have the years brought us closer together or farther apart?

30

Interviewing the Extended Family

Your extended family can give you unique insights on your parents and your upbringing. Through their stories you may come to understand your parents as never before. And you may find a new perspective on old pain and bewilderment.

Family get-togethers are a marvelous time for interviewing. A special trip just for that purpose usually provides welcome interest and entertainment. Don't procrastinate. Their memories are a resource you can lose. Contact them as quickly as possible and begin the process.

To increase your skills, you might want to pay special attention to the personality interviews you watch on TV. A warm smile, an inviting tone of voice, a little small talk help people to relax and feel at ease, and that is when memory works best.

What was Mother (Father) like when she (he) was little? Happy? Mischievous? Quiet? Did she have many friends? Was she clever with her hands? Was she smart? Obedient? Was she a reader? A tomboy?

When I was little did I remind you of her?

Was she a pretty teenager? Was she popular? Did she show early signs of having a good business head? Did she have a way of getting people to do what she wanted? Was she a hard worker? A rebel? Self-disciplined? Was she talented?

What was her relationship with her parents? Which parent do you think was her favorite? Why?

Did you approve of the way she was raised? Did she have all

the opportunities you would have wished for her?

Were the two of you close? What would she talk about? Was she shy in company? Did she laugh a lot?

When you first met, what did you think of my father (mother)? Did they have a tempestuous courtship? Do you think they were very much in love? What were some of the things they used to do together?

Did you dance at their wedding? Were you joyful or did you secretly feel sad? Worried? Was it a lovely wedding? Were their parents pleased?

Where did they honeymoon?

Can you remember when they first set up housekeeping? What kind of hostess was Mother? Did she have a job then?

Were they a happy couple? Did they fight a lot? Did they play a lot? Travel? Do you remember their favorite recreation when they were young? What about picnics and holidays?

Do you remember them as keeping to themselves or usually part of a group of friends?

Did they live mostly one life or two different lives?

What was my father doing for a living? Did he show promise? Did he enjoy his work?

Where were they living when I came along? Were they excited? Do you know where I was born? Did you see me when I was still an infant? When I was baptized?

Do you remember them being active in their community? In their church?

Did my parents have to struggle in those early days? How did they manage? Could they afford a car? Did anyone in the family help them? Did they need help?

Did Mother do all the housework herself? Did she pride herself on her housekeeping skills? What did Dad do around the house? Was he a good handyman?

Were there many family get-togethers in those days? What were they like?

How did my parents get along with the rest of their family? Who was their favorite relative?

Of the two, who was the boss? How did that suit the other? Did they quarrel much?

How do you think they got along with each other? Were they very much in love? Did they make a good team?

Do you think they enjoyed being parents? Did we kids slow them down? Which of us do you think was their favorite child? Were they harder on one of us than on the others? What would my parents say about me?

Did Mother (Father) complain much? About what? Did she laugh? Sing? Argue? Get excited? Was she happy?

What did you think of my parents as parents? As relatives? Do you think I'm pretty much the same kind of parent they were?

Can you remember what I was like as a small child? As a teenager? Was I a loner? Did I like to cuddle? Was I active? A dreamer?

Did I change much in personality and character as I grew up? Did the way I turned out surprise you?

31

Thoughts about the Twentieth Century

Here is a chance to express yourself about the events of our time. Choose a few and let yourself go . . . You might have a whole book of essays here! What are your thoughts about:

The beginning of this century. Clothing styles. Manners. Customs. Work. School. Ethics. Religion.

The First World War. What do you remember about it? How was your life affected?

The Roaring Twenties. The Charleston. Flappers.

Prohibition. Do you feel the same way about it now that you did when you were young?

Charles Lindbergh crossing the Atlantic in his tiny plane, The Spirit Of St. Louis.

The Stock Market Crash of 1929. The Great Depression.

Herbert Hoover vs. Franklin D. Roosevelt. Where were your (or your family's) sympathies?

The New Deal. How did you (or your family) feel about it?

Where you were on Pearl Harbor Day? What was your reaction? Any stories about World War II you haven't already discussed? D-Day, V-E Day, V-J Day? The day Roosevelt died.

Hiroshima. What was its significance to you at the time? Has it changed?

What was World War II's effect on the U.S.?

How has life changed since the War? What's better about our

present times? What's worse? What would you change if you could?

Who do you think was the best president of this century? What might have happened if some presidential elections had turned out differently?

Significant political changes. When? How did they come about?

The Soviet Union and the Cold War. Nuclear disarmament.

The United Nations.

The McCarthy Era. The Kennedy Years. The Nixon Era.

Changes in the economy . . . periods of recession and prosperity. What needs to be done to turn around our economy now? Is it possible?

Assassinations: Gandhi, Kennedy, King . . .

The rise of the Third World nations.

The space program.

The Vietnam war and its effect on the United States.

Developments in medicine, from antibiotics to transplants.

Technology . . . from Lindbergh to supersonic travel to computers to SDI.

Nuclear energy and its effect on the world.

Are there other political, economic, or technical developments that are of particular interest to you?

And then there were all those social changes. You must have an opinion about:

The Civil Rights Movement. Have we made progress? Enough progress?

The extended family. The nuclear family.

The new patterns of living.

The women's movement and the changes it brought. Has it helped women? Would you go back to the way it was before the women's movement? What changes still need to be made?

Working mothers. Single parents.

Changes in personal and family values.

The Sexual Revolution. The abortion question. AIDS.

Alcohol and drugs — why are we a nation of users?

Religion.

Recreation — from radio to video games.

The health and exercise movement.

Changes in communication and travel from telegraph to satellite.

Computer technology.

Education — why aren't we doing better by our kids?

Social Security — why aren't we doing better by our senior citizens?

The environment — do you think we have a problem?

The arts — music, literature, painting, drama — do you think they should be subsidized?

How do you think the 20th century will be judged?

The 21st century is almost upon us. What do you hope for it? What changes will it bring to your family? What can we do to make it a better century than the one we've known?

Part III
The Writing

32

Using Your Notes

The step from a bunch of notes to a finished story isn't as big as you might think. It'll take work, but you'll find the work absorbing.

Read your notes about the incident or person you've chosen to write about and then sit back for a bit and play with your memories. Let your feelings become involved in the process. They are more reliable in producing a good read than compilations of accurate data. Don't worry about grammar and spelling as you write. At this point how the story reads, capturing the images and incidents, is more important than whether every "i" is dotted or your sentences are grammatically correct.

Suppose, for example, that you decided to write the story of your first job, jerking sodas in a small town drugstore in the early 1950s.

Your notes describe the store. As you go over them you can picture the shelved walls, stacked with strange bottles and boxes — one of them reads Lydia Pinkham's Vegetable Compound — the row of high swivel stools, the long wooden counter with its two-gallon glass containers of Green River and Orange Delight.

Thinking about it, you can recall where the flavored syrups were kept and the powdered malt and mixers. You can picture yourself behind the counter mixing your specialty, the definitive chocolate soda. You remember hustling to keep up with the after school crowd, wisecracking back, flirting a little, watching the door, hoping that Mary Jo would stop in.

The store was owned by an old married couple — probably in their late thirties, you now realize. Try to focus in on them. Yes, she was tall and wore her dark hair in a bun. Not bad looking for someone that old. She was very businesslike and you were a little afraid of her. Her husband was tall and easygoing, and remember how he happened to hire you?

You have a hard time seeing his face and you can't dredge up either of their names. Don't worry about it. The names will come later, pop into your mind at some unexpected moment. If they never do, you can deal with it by admitting frankly, "I no longer remember their names, but . . ." Or you can rechristen them.

Focus on how they "felt" to you, what you thought about them. Most important, try to bring back the timidity and uncertainty of the moment when you faced them. They knew you as a customer, buying a soda, running an errand for your parents. Now you face them as a reluctant employee with nothing to recommend you except a brave smile.

If you can feel the tightness in your throat and the knot in your stomach that first day on the job, begin writing there — about the knot and how your hands were cold and some of your words didn't come out quite right and how Mr. Whatever-his-name looked down at you silently, not smiling when you asked what he wanted you to do.

If you don't remember what he said after he inspected your work, if everything is a dark blank after that terrible pause, write about that. You'll be surprised how well it will work in your story — warm, disarming, conveying your nervousness and discomfort more aptly than a word-by-word transcript of that day.

And now that you're into the scene, go with it. Write whatever comes to mind as rapidly as possible. Don't worry when the incidents become disjointed, not touching each other chronologically with great gaping holes of material left out. This isn't a debriefing for the military.

Drift through memories of your drugstore days, catching incidents and personalities: the time Mr. Anderson — oh, yes, that was his name — sent you up a ladder to dust the topmost shelves where the old-fashioned remedies with their arcane labels, laxatives — awful sounding stuff — liniments, "kidney remedies," hernia belts, all kinds of bottles claiming to relieve prostate problems and "women's troubles": Mr. Anderson told you they were mostly alcohol and coloring. Or the time one of the customers wanted you to sign his wife's name on an income tax refund. Or the "committee" of towns-people who entered the store demanding Mr. Anderson re-fuse service to the Japanese railroad workers and what he said to them.

All this may take a day or a week. It doesn't matter; each writer has his own pace. When you are getting started again on the second day, you may want to read over your first day's work to get in the mood. Fine, but don't tinker with the story unless it is to insert some new memory. People who begin re-vising their stories too early, often never finish. They write and rewrite a few paragraphs, a few pages, again and again, trying for perfection — and, of course, nothing is ever perfect — until finally they become discouraged with themselves as writers and abandon the project.

On the other hand, when you write until the end of your story, you have the pride of completion. You've done it. An entire story. You weren't certain you could, but you did. A story. *Your* story. You've gained confidence in yourself as a writer.

As you write, more and more about the store will surface. you'll hear the bell jangling when the door opened, smell the stinging harshness of liniment, visualize the pharmacy. in back and the cash register over at the side. And the faces of customers, the wheelers and dealers, and the beautiful woman with the big stomach and no husband that people talked about in whispers.

For most people memory scenes don't come in a large comprehensive overview but, as in dreams, bits and pieces surface at different times. Often a flash of memory will come as you work that doesn't fit into the story you're telling. Write it down anyway, indented so it sticks out from the rest or box it in colored ink for easy recognition, and go on with your story. At some later date you can go back to that nota-tion and find the spot that cries out for it.

Feel the sense of accomplishment and pleasure now you have a completed story. It's much more satisfying than a half dozen beginnings and partially completed stories. Now you know you can do it. And you have something to share with your family.

Once you have written an entire story from beginning to

end, you'll find writing the next one easier. You gain in skill and confidence as you work from completed story to completed story.

How long should it be? A good completed story can be only a page long or it can be as long as thirty pages. It isn't the length that makes it a completed story, but the sense of satisfaction, the feeling that you have said everything you wanted to say. Less wouldn't have been enough; more would be padding. That's the right length for a story.

33

After You Have Finished

All right, in your first draft you've finished writing everything you have to say about your drugstore days. What do you have? It could be a short story complete in itself. It could be a chapter in what eventually will be a full-length autobiography. It could be the beginning of a short memoir on your adolescence. It could be the first in a series of short stories, all related to your personal history. It depends entirely on you.

What do you want? How far do you want to go?

You may have discovered that you love working with ideas and words, that there really is a writer inside you just waiting to be released. If you have discovered the writer, you will do your best work by exploring the writer's needs.

Don't be anxious if you are not certain at this point whether you want to work on a full-length book or a collection of short pieces. The chances are you'll have to write considerably more than one piece before your interests and ambition settle on specific goals. At this point concentrate on discovering your needs in terms of motivation and gaining self-confidence. Some writers work best by taking small bites and chewing them thoroughly. Try staying with "Drugstore Days," rewriting it, polishing it, honing it to your satisfaction, before tackling another incident. Then when you've finished the first draft of that second story, try going on immediately to a new story. And perhaps after that begin the first draft of another story.

How do you feel? Are you gaining momentum and energy as you move from one first draft to another? Perhaps you don't have the patience for perfecting and polishing. You may be driven by a need to get your stories on paper as fast as you can so they won't be lost. If you don't want to bother with rewriting at this point, don't look back. Put "Drugstore Days" aside and begin another story, perhaps about the same age period on another theme — some camping experiences or your first baby. Go for it. Write in first draft until you have said all you want to say on that theme. Then when no more stories come to mind, that will be the time to go back and begin your revision.

But you may feel uneasy and unsure, muddled and disorganized about your first draft work. If you feel apologetic, as though you weren't really a writer because the first draft work wasn't finished, then you should rewrite and polish as you go along so that each story is ready to show off before you begin the next.

The choice is yours. The only criterion is which approach gives you the most energy and the most confidence in yourself as a writer.

You'll find suggestions for revising your material in the next section.

Or if you wish to hold off on revision until you have a finished work complete with Table of Contents, look at the section on Putting Your Book Together. There you will find directions on how to make a book out of a bunch of short stories.

34

Improving Your Stories

DESIGN

The design of your story is the first decision to be made in revising. Where do you begin, where do you end, how do you tell what should be in the middle.

In your first draft, you gambled on a beginning and went on from there. That beginning *may* introduce your material to its best advantage. But read your story over again carefully, asking yourself if there isn't another place that would be more inviting, more compelling, more amusing as an opening.

For example, in "Drugstore Days," you started in the present and flashed back to when you were sixteen, playing mumblety-peg. Opening with a flashback can be exciting. But there are other possibilities. You could begin with yourself high up on that ladder, reading the labels of the old-time nostrums and, occasionally, dusting. That was when you have Mr. Anderson calling up to you, "Shake a leg! School lets out in only half an hour." In describing him, the kind of boss he was, you could then go back to your first impressions that day when he hired you, and after that, onward to the noisy excitement of your classmates' daily invasion of the drugstore.

The same approach to design holds for your story's conclusion. With what thought, with what feeling do you want to leave your readers? Look for the incident, the comment that creates the effect best.

How would you end your story using this new beginning? In a logical design, you would end with the day you quit your job to go on to the university.

But you might want something with more punch. You might choose to end with Mr. Anderson standing up to the townspeople: "Those Japanese railroad workers are welcome in my store, and if you don't like it, you'll just have to get your drugs elsewhere."

Before that moment Mr. Anderson had been just another adult to me, someone who could be a resource, but was also something of a threat — basically uninteresting, old and stodgy. But watching him take a stand that could have hurt his business, suddenly I understood that Mr. Anderson was a big man.

You could end there and let your readers take your point themselves. Or you could decide to highlight your point by concluding: And I realized that being a druggist could be more than following a tiresome routine twelve hours a day. Its responsibilities could give you the ability to make a difference in your community.

Once you have your beginning and your ending, you'll want to shape your middle portion to support these decisions. You can do this by continuing from your beginning with interesting incidents that carry out your theme. You will be describing personalities and relationships that will build up to your ending logically or contrast with it in a spurt of surprise.

Don't be surprised if halfway through one approach you decide on another. Professional writers frequently change structure mid-course. You *could* start your story with the daily high school attack on the soda fountain, or with your saying goodbye to Mr. Anderson, and then working backward to being hired. The possibilities are limited only by the number of incidents and one's imagination. As you work and re-work your material, you uncover them.

When one of your stories turns stubborn on you, and no matter how you twist it about, it just lies there awkwardly, try a little research. Read some short stories, and notice how your favorite authors handle their beginnings, middles, and endings. A writer can't hide his trade secrets; they are right there on the page for anyone to use. Structuring an entire book involves the same principles: where to begin, where to end, and how to bridge the gap most effectively.

Many writers are content to use time as a skeleton for their structure. They begin an autobiography with their birth and go forward to present time (as we have structured our questions in this book). Or they begin their memoirs with the first chronological incident in that period and continue through to its last incident. This approach worked wonders for James Herriot in *All Creatures Great and Small.*

Your material itself will exert considerable influence on your decision. If its beginning seems slow, you will want to look for more intriguing possibilities. Assuming a book's worth of material for *Drugstore Days*, you might want to start off behind the counter making a soda. Each customer becomes a separate portrait and recalls another incident — its own chapter. A humorous memoir might use your blunders and Mr. Anderson's reprimands as the organizing structure, with disaster building on disaster. Essentially that was the structure of the hilarious British television series "Fawlty Towers" or the American "I Love Lucy" series.

Probably nobody has written up petty disasters to greater delight than James Thurber in *My Life and Hard Times.* And if you read his collection of mishaps, take heart and gather confidence by noticing from what a small scattering of memories that marvelous book was created. Another satisfactory opening for your book would be an essay about your town, describing its environment and layout, its lines of influence and power, its network of social organizations, how people earn their livings, building to the drugstore's place in the scheme of things.

If you're interested in the women's movement, you could structure your book to various kinds of relationships involving women. You could demonstrate Mrs. Anderson's strength and administrative abilities, showing her having to execute them through her relaxed and laid-back husband. You would build on this theme by selecting and emphasizing incidents that showed men's power and the townswomen's need to manipulate, to pretend. You could choose incidents that would show them sublimating their energies and resentments in trivialities, hypochondria, and patent medicine addiction. *The Woman Warrior* by Maxine Hong Kingston is an example of a fascinating ethnic memoir that makes a powerful statement.

You could make *Drugstore Days* illustrate small town

politics as symbolized by the never-ending, angry battles over the local water district — farmers against townspeople — argued and schemed between slurps of Green River and bites of apple pie and ice cream.

Or if you choose to emphasize the values and decency of the town, you could start with the way the town mobilized against its first serious criminal.

WORD CHOICE AND RHYTHM

Word choice may sound like another way to say vocabulary test, but it isn't. Usually the best words for personal histories are part of everyday speech.

It isn't new or difficult words or elegant words that are needed, but those that come from the heart and your own thought patterns. For instance, if you were recording your early dislike of Brussels sprouts, you could focus on their color — "they rolled around on my plate, green, like a disease."

Or their smell — "Mom had a way of making creamed Brussels sprouts look all right, but their stench gagged me."

The trick to word choice is reliving the event before describing it and then reading your words to see how well they call up what you saw and felt in memory. If those words don't quite make it, have another go. What *did* Brussels sprouts taste like? Bland? Bitter? Musty? What best suggests your revulsion — Mold? Fungus? Disease? Play with the possibilities until one satisfies — that's your word choice.

Reading your material — aloud is best — helps the process enormously. As you read, your ear will tell you if you have repeated a word or phrase monotonously — or whether repetition created the emphasis you wanted.

And only reading your sentences will reveal whether the words you have strung together produce rhythms that work for or against your purposes.

Ordinarily, you will want a smooth, even flow of words for your storytelling. However, used deliberately, uneven, jarring rhythms create tension, underscoring and supporting your word choice. Fast-paced rhythms can help you create a sense of hurry or confusion; slow powerful beats build an impression of deliberation or, with different word choices, of easy sensuality.

Rhythm will help you heat up a scene from indifference to irritation to fury or from unease to anxiety to panic. You can show a family Thanksgiving get-together moving from the moment of spick-and-span perfection just before the arrival of the first guest to a chaos of intersecting movement and chatter culminating in The Meal, and slowly subsiding to satiated drowsiness.

No one can teach you better than your own ear. Read your favorite authors slowly so that your ear catches their tricks with rhythm. You've been learning the uses of rhythm casually throughout your lifetime as you listened and read. You come to the project already trained. You only need some concentrated conscious effort to complete the process.

VOICE

Have you ever noticed that some people say a great deal of nothing at all, but they say it so pleasantly that you become a willing listener. That's how a persuasive narrative voice works in writing. Some writers can catch and hold you by voice alone. Others, good writers too, grate in their narrative voice and if they didn't tell such a good story, with such interesting characters, you'd put down the book.

An inviting narrative voice is worth trying for. But the process of acquiring one is difficult to describe. Your attitude when writing has a lot to do with it. A cheerful confidence that what you have to say is going to interest and a warm regard for your prospective reader are a good part of the secret. Kipling in *The Just So Stories* is the ultimate in narrative voice: small children snuggle up to it; adults never outgrow it. Written for *his* children, his open affection and his confidence that he could capture their imagination with his fantasies made magic.

Somerset Maugham had an engaging narrative voice, and Daphne du Maurier (read the opening lines of *Rebecca*) and Evelyn Waugh and Robertson Davies and Muriel Sparks. But listen as you read and make your own list. Reading authors with inviting narrative voices is catching. Their boldness and energy, their confiding tone get under your skin; you become infected with some of their talent.

For the rest of the process, working on your narrative voice is a matter of getting a good night's sleep and attacking your project enthusiastically in the spirit of adventure. We can't all charm birds out of trees with voice alone, but it is amazing what a little relaxed practice will achieve.

DESCRIPTION

Probably more people have given up on writing over their first attempts at description than any other single difficulty . . . unless it's dialogue.

The problem with description is that it's impossible. No one really can adequately describe anything so that someone who has never seen it is likely to recognize it at a chance encounter.

Gather a bunch of leaves from different plants and try to describe them so that your neighbor could match description to leaf. Not an easy assignment, and notice when you've done how dull the descriptions are. Identification of objects is not the true purpose of literary description.

In a recent mystery from his Rabbi Small series, Harry Kemelman described an important character as "a little pot-bellied man with a round head, which was balding and rimmed with sparse, mouse-colored hair." Look around any shopping center and count the men who could fit those words. And Pat Conroy, whose descriptions in *The Prince of Tides* lure readers to the South Carolina coastline, doesn't intend that you use his novel in place of a map and guidebook. He wanted his readers to feel the wild beauty and mystery of that ragged seacoast. So he formed his descriptions to call up emotion much more than relay photographic scenes.

Effective descriptions are written to evoke emotion and attitude with only a few clue words to summon pictures in your mind from your experience. Suppose you wanted to describe the dog that came wandering out of the desert into the drugstore one hot afternoon: Two wary eyes stared out of the mass of matted gray fur. The size of the dog inspired Mrs. Anderson to wave a broom at him and it wasn't until he'd begun to turn away that she noticed the limp in his walk.

Now there isn't enough information there to pick Frenchie out of an animal shelter, far less to let the reader know that Frenchie was a French Briard. But the dog's breed isn't as important to the story as the emotion it evokes. Almost everyone has seen a dog that's been kicked around by life and is the worse for it. That's the feel, the image you're trying to call up and those words will trigger your reader's memory of such a dog and create the feelings that will make them respond to your story.

The trick about descriptions is not only to remember sight, smell, feel, and sound, but to let yourself feel once again how you felt about what you are describing at the time of your story. The specifics to write down are those that best symbolize and evoke those feelings.

Your own memories fit in well with this approach because the chances are you will have forgotten much information that is nonessential to your descriptions. There are those fortunate few whose memory seems literally to film experience for later replay. Most of us have memories that are less complete and exact. And what we "see" again, "hear," "taste," "feel," again or remember as concepts are the aspects of the past that most impressed us, to our pleasure or dismay. The dull and unimportant soon fade away. Fortunately, your tantalizingly incomplete memories will provide you with exactly what best can be worded into effective description.

How lean, how lush you make your descriptions depends on your preferences and style. What descriptions by other writers work best on you? That's the approach you'll be happiest with in your own writing. Of course, it won't be an exact duplicate of another writer's work — and you wouldn't want it to be — your own personality and viewpoint will infuse differences that make your adopted style uniquely your own.

CHARACTERIZATION

Transmitting personality to paper requires a special alchemy. People are more than three dimensional; they have more sides to their nature than the most complex crystal. Not only is it impossible to squeeze all of any person's many facets into a paragraph or a short story, you wouldn't want to try. People usually have only a couple of facets showing at a time. If you know your characters at all well, you know more about them than was in evidence in the incident you are writing about.

Don't try to tell everything you know at once. Remember you didn't learn everything you know about your friends at once. Part of our fascination with people is the thrill of discovery. Use that fascination, that thrill in your characterization. Show a bit about your characters in one incident, then a bit more in the next incident, later add something else. Your readers will enjoy the sense of exploring, of discovery, and they will think how lifelike these characters are!

The different views add depth to your material and keep it exciting. Louise Erdrich's *Love Medicine* is a superb example of how people can be revealed little by little, first by one narrator, then another, through different incidents occurring at different times.

Sometimes you will want to characterize through narration: Mrs. Anderson had an inner reserve that could chill you to the bone.

Sometimes you will want to characterize by showing your character in action: Counting out her money, Sally Perkins leaned closer over the counter, confidentially. "That Ligatt girl can't go on claiming her big stomach is just some extra pounds much longer. All that riding around on a motorcycle. I guess she's hoping to get rid of it."

Mrs. Anderson accepted the money without comment and rang it up; then looking directly at Sally Perkins, she said, "You must spend a lot of your time sitting on your front porch doing nothing but watching other people's business, Sally."

Mr. Anderson always backed up Mrs. Anderson. After Sally Perkins huffed out of the store. Mrs. Anderson went over to him and said, "I just lost us another customer." And he laughed and gave her a squeeze. "Let her drive the nine miles over to Penton's for a while. It'll give us a rest from her tongue."

The two techniques work well together. Which you use the most depends on which you're best at. It also depends on your space. Notice how much longer it takes to reveal character in action. On the other hand it's more convincing. Rather than being told, readers are able to draw their own conclusions. And that's always more satisfying.

DIALOGUE

How good you will be at dialogue depends on your ear for music.

People don't talk alike. Even people in the same small town have different patterns of speech, different tonal ranges, different rhythms, different word choices. Of course you don't want to reproduce speech exactly — it would be boring. We don't even listen to each other fully; we "tune each other out" as our mind scampers off on thoughts of our own, while our dearest chum chatters on with a story we're hearing for the third time.

The trick to dialogue is to keep the flavor of the spoken word but weed out enough of its repetitions, hesitations, digressions to make it endurable.

Again your ear will be your best guide. After you've pruned your character's words, read over the results. Does it sound like Mr. Anderson?

Perfection in dialogue would be making it so distinctive that without attribution, your reader knows who is speaking. Even the best writers rarely achieve that perfection. But distinctive differences in speech can be transferred to the page with practice by those with an ear for dialogue.

If, though you've practiced and practiced and even though Mr. Anderson's Norwegian beginnings show in his speech in your story, he still reads like the Ligatt woman or like a third-rate comedian trying to imitate a Norwegian dialect, don't despair. You *can* be a good writer without being good at dialogue. Just use it less and lean harder on narration.

Those of you who can make a page read like people talking, rejoice. Eavesdropping on private conversations is one of the joys of reading. Dialogue will make your stories sparkle with interest and the feeling of authenticity. Tell your readers in narration that Sally Perkins was a stingy, contentious neighbor and they will ask themselves what you have against the woman. But have the Ligatt woman tell Mrs. Anderson that after scrubbing all day to clean up Sally's kitchen to a semblance of decency, Sally argued about her taking a half hour for lunch and then only paid three quarters of her price and your readers will tell themselves that Sally is contentious and stingy.

Practicing dialogue is a great out-of-house games. Standing in lines becomes a joy and resource. Listen to what's being said around you and try to convert it into dialogue.

In your writing focus on the sides of your character that show in the incident. The other sides of the person will emerge in other incidents.

And while you're entertaining yourself, work on attributions as well. Often they are the least appealing part of dialogue: He said, she said. He/she laughed, hissed, snorted, roared, purred, squeaked, whined, bellowed, shouted, gurgled, yelled, whispered, murmured. He said gruffly. With bold accusation in her eye, she said. Coarsely, he told her. Running up to him, she skidded to a halt and put her hands behind her back. "Oh, Hank," she whispered. "It's been so long."

Attributions require deft handling. Usually you want them to disappear into the page, serving only as signposts to indicate who is talking. Repetitions of he said/she said are better than overuse of the more dramatic verbs of attribution. Occasionally, it becomes important to your story to suggest a tone of voice, behavior, or emotion connected to speech. Then use one of the specialized verbs, perhaps giggled or whimpered or a clause — he said hesitantly. Or perhaps you'll do your indicating without direct attributions — He looked at her and hesitated. "Mike's dead. He died this morning."

With attributions, it's your eye that tells you whether you've tried too hard to be fresh and distinctive or have leaned backwards into too many lean, dry, uncommunicative repetitions of he said, she said.

HOW LONG?

THE SENTENCE — The length really should depend on

what you want the sentence to do. You can squeeze a lot of information into one long sentence that would take even longer and seem more tedious written in several sentences. On the other hand, readers can get lost in very long sentences, especially of the rambling sort — try it and see! — and too many long sentences can lose your reader's attention. Short sentences attract attention: Look out! Watch me. Here I come! They add energy to your paragraph. But short sentences can jar. They should be short for a purpose. You don't want to sound like a machine gun.

Let you ear guide you when to change from long to short. The more you write and read your material, the more you examine other writers' sentences, the stronger and more certain your instincts will become for patterns and length.

THE PARAGRAPH — Paragraphs usually focus on a thought. New thought, new paragraph. Too long a paragraph can act like a wall, discouraging further progress. If your paragraph gets of a size to make your readers feel they need a compass and a flashlight to find their way through it, breaking it up would be a kindness. Furthermore, the white space around short paragraphs lightens up the material and makes it easier to read.

One-sentence paragraphs are workhorses.

They add emphasis. They attract attention. They add a thoughtful pause to your pace of prose, ideas, and action. If you really want punch, you can go further than that.

Wow!

A one-word paragraph, like chili pepper, isn't something you want to overuse. But it does pep up a page. And it gives an importance to "Wow" that it wouldn't have inside a longer paragraph.

Of course, in dialogue you can indicate change of speaker with a new paragraph.

"Why is this paragraph so long, John?"

"Because, Mary, that's the length it is."

Often writers will use this technique when they want to emphasize what is being said without surrounding it with description or narration.

If you use an attribution, you don't need a new paragraph to show the change of speaker. The attribution accomplishes that, and using attribution, you can have several characters speaking in the same paragraph.

Puzzled, she looked up, asking, "John, why is this sentence so long?" Striding to the window to cover his annoyance, he opened it and peered out before replying, "Because that's the length it is."

STORY — Just where the short story becomes a novelette and a novelette becomes a novella and a novella becomes a novel can be the start of a fine literary wrangle.

A short short story can be one page long. Short stories usually come in about five to ten double-spaced pages but twenty pages wouldn't be unseemly. At about thirty pages we enter the middle kingdom of the novelette; and fifty pages, the novella. A novel can be as short as a hundred pages; most continue on to two and three hundred. Over four hundred starts getting heavy to hold. Perhaps you should consider Volume II.

Memoirs are usually novel length. Autobiographies tend to be long. Can four hundred pages tell it all? Currently we are seeing more people write their personal histories as a series of short stories or memoirs covering different incidents and periods of their lives than attempting the full assault on the non-stop autobiography.

The less heroic bite of the autobiographical short story is certainly easier for the writer to chew, and for most readers it makes a more tasty mouthful.

The fun of writing is that you get to choose. Don't feel you have to follow the herd. If you want to tackle twelve volumes, 700 pages each, of autobiographical saga, attack!

PUNCTUATION

Punctuation is changing year by year. And with punctuation your reading can lead you astray. Some novels and non-fiction books being published exhibit less than standard punctuation and many books on the market are British, with rules that differ somewhat from American English.

How nice you want to be in punctuation depends on your purposes and personality. If you enjoy informality, don't worry about punctuation beyond the needs of being understood. If you take pleasure in being "correct," you might want to brush up by looking into a good *recent* manual — perhaps The University of Chicago's *Manual Of Style* or Pinkert's *Practical Grammar.*To get you started here are a few models of accepted ways of punctuating the most common sentence structures. All of them are acceptable.

There are twelve marks of punctuation to consider: the semicolon (;) the colon (:) the dash (—) the question mark (?) the exclamation point (!) the quotation marks (") invariably used in pairs, the single quotation mark (') also always used in pairs, the apostrophe (') which looks like a single quotation mark and uses the same key on the typewriter, the parentheses (), ellipses (. . .), used to indicate trailing or interrupted speech and thought, and the comma (,), and finally the period (.) which ends most sentences.

If you have a question about your work, with luck you'll find the model you need among them.

Punctuation can be used to clarify and emphasize meaning and regulate the speed of your prose.

Punctuation can be used to clarify, emphasize meaning, and regulate the speed of your prose.

However useful, punctuation is a vexation. If you want to defy punctuation, read E.L. Doctorow's *Loon Lake* and be encouraged.

If you want to defy punctuation read E.L. Doctorow's *Loon Lake* and be encouraged.

Fortunately for our purposes punctuation isn't difficult. You can pick up what you need quickly.

Fortunately, for our purposes, punctuation isn't difficult; you can pick up what you need quickly.

Fortunately for our purposes punctuation isn't difficult, and you can pick up what you need quickly.

Do pick up what you need, but fortunately for our purposes punctuation isn't difficult.

When you master commas, you have gone two-thirds of the way to mastering the art of punctuation.

You have gone two thirds of the way to mastering the art of punctuation when you have mastered commas: I finally mastered commas, although I had to get a whip and gun to do it.

After ten minutes, my eyes began crossing.

After ten minutes my eyes began crossing.

Wearing a punk hairdo and a billowing dress, Karen looked more like a hurricane on legs than a bookie.

He took a sip from his bottle "for courage," and then he took another sip to help the first sip.

He took a sip from his bottle "for courage" and then he took another sip to help the first sip.

Then he looked from his page of words to his box of commas; I've got to combine you, he thought, but how?

Calling Karen Blackheart, his bookie, he asked, "How many commas should I put into my first page, kid?"

"You still owe me for that question on dashes," Karen told him coldly.

"But, Karen, baby," he pleaded. "I need the information now. Tell me and I'll send you a tenner next week."

"But . . . I need it now," he pleaded.

"Go get your manuscript," she said, her index finger dancing over a hand-held calculator. "This will cost you interest. Twelve percent."

"This will cost you interest: twelve percent."

"This will cost you interest — twelve percent."

"This will cost you interest, twelve percent."

"Commas! Harry cried. "How many of them?"

"You don't use them by number," Karen told him.

"How then?"

"By rules. There's not much logic to it, only custom."

"Can't you just tell me how many and let me sprinkle them in?"

"No, you'll have to read me the sentences. Believe me, this is gonna cost you, Harry."

"Believe me — this is gonna cost you."

"All right, I've got the manuscript in my hand."

"All right I've got the manuscript in my hand."

"Sit down and read."

"Sit down, and read."

So Harry sat down with his manuscript on his lap (it was heavy and the pages kept slipping out and fluttering to the floor) and, holding the telephone to his ear with one hand and underlining sentences with the index finger of his other hand, he began reading.

"Harry . . . um . . . er . . . wait! You're already shy a comma. You need one after *oh* — though you never use a comma after *O*, as in O Lord protect me — Sorry, but that's the way it is."

"You want me to write, 'oh, hell'? Well I won't do it. The fellows would laugh at me."

Karen sighed. "I'm telling you, Harry. 'oh, hell' is better. But some of these skimpy young punctuaters are leaving it out. If you must, leave it at 'oh hell,' but my fee just went up." (And as she spoke, she jotted down a reminder to have Harry remove her name from his Acknowledgment Page.)

STYLE

Discussions of style can be daunting, and certain people — critics, teachers, your most intimate friends — deliberately use the word to intimidate. Is *your* style up to snuff? With all the pretense and status-climbing boiled out, style comes down to your personality in writing. Getting you into your writing is more important than any of the rules.

Oh, you may not want your written work to come out like you in your grungy jeans and old sneakers, bolting down a quick sandwich over the kitchen sink. So you practice the various elements of writing we have discussed and you read other writers to learn some new tricks, much in the same way you might buy some new clothes for an important occasion.

If the process of writing intrigues you, you may even sign up for a writing class or go to a writer's conference. But always the essence of what you are doing is expressing *you*, your life, your personality, your view of events, your emotional range, your feel for language — we think you'll like the adventure of seeing yourself and your world take shape on paper, become permanent, solid, something to point to, something to give, a chronicle of who you are and what you accomplished.

We're hoping you will become addicted to the process of writing; and that by the time you finish you'll be more than a personal historian, you will have become a writer.

35

Putting Your Book Together

At last you have all your writing in order. You've revised, corrected, and proofread it for spelling and other technical errors. Your stories are as colorful, interesting, and accurate as you can make them. You have nothing to add or delete.

You may want to submit your manuscript to a publishing house in hopes of a sale and, who knows, a best seller. You may want to contact one of the reputable businesses that will publish (and help distribute) your manuscript for you at your expense.

You can produce and publish your book yourself if you want. There are any number of self-publishing books on the market. Your public library probably has at least one that will show you how to get your manuscript typeset, printed, and bound, and then how to publicize and distribute it. Or you may want to buy a computer and the necessary software for desk-top publishing, which will allow you to do the expensive typesetting step yourself.

There is also a much less expensive and much more simple approach open to you: a largely handmade or typewritten book. The finished product can be handsome and lasting. Here's how to go about it: If you can afford it, buy enough of a good quality rag bond paper for the final draft of your book. You don't want the paper to turn brown or deteriorate. If you are writing by hand, have a large enough supply on hand of pens of the same point and color ink to finish the job so you won't have to change in the middle of your manuscript.

If you have decided to use an already bound journal or diary-type book, be sure it has satisfactory quality paper and enough pages. You want all this work to survive for a long time.

Is your book a continuous narrative, divided into chapters, or is it a series of short stories or vignettes about many different incidents? You could place them in chronological order, as this guide does. Or you might choose to group together by characters: all the stories about your mother, your spouse, your children, or your friends. Maybe you want to group them by subject: your career, your marriage, parenting, your ideas about the future. It's possible you find that you have a whole collection about one central theme, maybe, like Iacocca, your work, or like Bill Cosby, fatherhood. Perhaps you have an exciting collection of travel stories.

It's time to put your book together. Here's what you do. Leave the first page after the cover blank, this is called the end paper. Let's say you're writing "The Boothe Story." That title goes in the center of the second page (it's called the half-title).

Now for the title page. Of course, your title is centered about two-thirds down from the top. Do you have a subtitle? Maybe "Four Generations of an English Family in America." Put that below your title, and under that the author's name, yours. Your title page now looks like this:

THE BOOTHE STORY

Four Generations of an English Family in America

by

Marianne Boothe Sterling

On the back of the title page, write or type the word "Copyright" and the symbol c, followed by your name and the date. This is your notice of copyright, and ensures that no one else can appropriate, quote, change, or copy what you have written without your permission.

Your manuscript represents a great deal of work and you never can tell what will become of it. You may have created a fascinating, saleable book that someone will want to publish. This symbol states that you are the legal owner. Your copyright lasts all your life and belongs to your heirs for fifty years after that.

On the next page, write your dedication. This is your

chance to express love, gratitude, or any other personal message, usually to an individual.

Following this, write your introduction, telling your readers why you wrote your book, and what you hope they will get from it. If you are writing a family history, it would be interesting to do this by hand, even if the rest is typed. Handwriting is better than a photo in establishing a personal connection. You could do it in the form of a letter to those who will be reading your book. Can you imagine what such a personal message from someone in your own past would mean to you? In most books, the Table of Contents comes next. For personal histories, it isn't necessary unless you've given your stories titles and want to show them up front. If you make a Table of Contents, fill in the page numbers after you have completed the manuscript. Now, on the next right-hand page you begin your story. This is page one.

Copies of drawings, photographs, or documents can be inserted where they are mentioned in your story, or you can just put them all together in a separate section. Remember to use only copies of important documents or photos and make a note as to where the original can be found.

When you have finished, by all means, have copies made of your manuscript. The cost is usually less than ten cents a page, and many photocopiers now do such a fine job that, except for photographs, it is hard to tell the copy from the original. Some copy shops will print both sides of the page, assemble them in order, and bind them in a cover for a small additional charge. The final product looks almost like a professionally produced book, and you will have the thrill of seeing your work in print.

This book may be finished, but your story isn't. As long as you live, the story continues. There will always be exciting tales to tell, experiences, hopes, and dreams to share.

We wish you joy and success with your project, and hope it will be a rewarding adventure for you.

36

A Sampling of Personal Histories to Delight You

We're hoping you can make up your own reading list of personal histories. You personal history fans might want to inspect our list for goodies you overlooked. And, neophytes, prepare for a feast.

If you have ever wished for one more life to live, personal histories are for you.

If you peek into lighted windows as you walk down a street at night, personal histories are for you.

If your mind drifts away from a speaker's pomposity to speculations about his private life, personal histories are for you.

If you have been struck by disaster and are staggering under its weight, trying to cope, trying not to be crushed by bitterness or despondency, personal histories are for you.

If family drama affords you delicious amusement, which other members haven't the sense of humor to share, personal histories are for you.

If you feel there must be better ways of human interaction than those you see at home and work, personal histories are for you.

If you enjoy the human species despite its craziness or because of it, personal histories are for you.

If you thrill to courage, to adventure, to love, to the pursuit of knowledge, to generosity of spirit, to wisdom, personal histories are for you.

In addition to the entertainment they give us, other people's personal histories are packed with valuable hints for writing your own.

As you read, notice where they begin, how they bridge from one event to another, how they describe the people in their lives, what about them captures their interest. Notice how interesting are even the mundane details of other people's lives, how much can be made of how little. Notice how an incomplete, blurred memory translates into a good story.

Reading a great variety of personal histories allows you to discover what styles most appeal to you. They are your best guide.

Do you like the memoirs that are intimate? Do you like those that deal more with community life, environment, career, questions of ethics and philosophy?

What narrative voice pleases your ear, chatty, elegant, balanced and objective, romantic, down to earth? Soak up its style to infuse into your own.

What tone do you most admire, humorous, practical, confiding, scholarly, imposing? Dare to follow suit.

What organization of material captures your imagination, rambling and discursive, thematic, chronological? There is your model.

How open and revealing should you be? How reserved? Should you always put your best foot forward, hoping to conceal human weaknesses? Which do you prefer, Lord Chesterfield or James Herriot?

We have included some journals and one collection of letters because in time both become a kind of personal history, and both are valuable resources for writing a personal history.

Put out the word among family and friends for old letters from you that they have kept. You certainly will find their information useful; you may want to quote from them; you may even want to include them, whole cloth, in your project.

Our list isn't a feather's weight of the personal histories your neighborhood library has waiting for you. New ones are being published every season. Your enjoyment of old personal histories will suggest the dimensions of the legacy you are leaving your family. New ones give fresh perspectives on the times we have lived through. The differences in perspective are fascinating in themselves. Add your own to their number.

Reading personal histories will inspire to write your own. When your inspiration flags, read a few more.

Adams, Henry: His autobiographical account of intellectual development in an emerging country will give you some ideas of how to present the development of your own political, economic, and moral views.

Anderson, William: *Ancestors.* This study of a family's genealogy expands intriguingly to provide a glance at American history.

Arlen, Michael J.: *Passage to Ararat* is an account of the son of a famous novelist seeking his Armenian roots.

Antin, Mary: *The Promised Land,* first published in 1912 and republished in 1969, is an account of a young immigrant girl's struggles to express herself in a new language, and is particularly relevant today with our influx of immigrants. If you need proof of the value of recording your life, read this timeless memoir.

Aurelius, Marcus: *Meditations* is a book to give you confidence that your observations of your times will have relevance for generations undreamed of.

Bacall, Lauren: *By Myself,* an autobiography by a New York Jewish girl who was an usher when she was discovered by a modeling agency, describes her career, her private life and demonstrates that honesty in straightforward prose can be disarming.

Baker, Russell: In *Good Times, New York Times* columnist Russell Baker uses humor and openness to show the man at work, and the work shaping the man. Stories about your career are of particular interst to family and non-work friends. It's new territory, a side of you they have never been able to meet.

Growing Up, his memoir about his early years during the Depression, is delightful, funny, touching, *and* won a Pulitzer Prize.

Burton, Sir Richard F.: *Personal Narrative of a Pilgrimage to Medina and Mecca* is a famous travel account by a Westerner who disguised himself as an Arab to visit the forbidden holy cities of the Moslem world. An excellent example of travel writing, description of terrain and local customs. Burton is still being read because his Medina and Mecca are no more.

Chernin, Kim: *In My Mother's House* deals with growing

up in the forties and fifties in the home of Communist parents. A daughter's honest and loving account of a difficult childhood.

Lord Chesterfield: *Lord Chesterfield's Letters to His Son and Others.* Written in the 19th century, these letters are still being read for their comments on ethical and philosophical issues.

Churchill, Winston: *My Early Life*, a charming memoir, written by Churchill before he launched into the important part of his life. Take note: no matter how young you are or how much you plan to accomplish, it's not too soon to begin your personal history.

Cousins, Norman: There is nothing wrong with talking about your aches, pains, and fears of disease. Look what this author did for all of us with his *Anatomy of an Illness*.

Crevecoeur, Hector St. John: *Diary of an American Farmer*

Darwin, Charles: *The Voyage of the Beagle* is an account of the trip that changed our civilization's view of all life forms. In addition to being one of the most important documents in the history of humanity, it is an engaging story written by a shy fundamentalist who had an overweening curiosity and intellectual honesty which led him to be the most reluctant Darwinist of all. Your family knows you as breadwinner and parent, as someone hovering into middle age and, as they once said of Helen Trent, even beyond. Although the trip itself and Darwin's observations hold our interest, even more it is the young Darwin himself who captures our imagination.

Day, Clarence: *Life with Father* may suggest ways of treating your own feelings of ambivalence with grace yet honesty about a somewhat overbearing parent. Its humor not only entertains, it packages the events in a form that was comfortable to the writer and his family.

de Tocqueville, Alexis: *Democracy in America* was written about 1840. This personal look at the United States by a French nobleman and political historian is still being read. At once charming, insightful, and farseeing, this account of our country as it emerged from its revolutionary beginnings shows the value of a look at transitions. At this moment the world around us is being shaken by one of the greatest economic and political revolutions of all time. A record of observations can provide insights and entertainment that may earn an equal life span.

Dinesen, Isak: _Out of Africa_ was written a great distance of time from the events described, after the writer had become a quite different person from the young woman who tried to farm in Africa. Biographical research reveals that the author freely mixed fiction in with her fact, just as she wrote under a pen name rather than use her legal name, Karen Blixen. For all its fictions, the memoir is rich in psychological truths, an honest perspective that is more important than mere information.

Fisher, M.F.K.: _Sister Age_ is a rich collection and excellent guide for those who prefer to write separate to one long narrative.

Franklin, Benjamin: _The Autobiography of Benjamin Franklin_ is a personal history that set a moral stamp on generations of Americans. This mixture of private experience and philosophy illustrates the value of personal history as a window to bygone times.

Faulkner, William: His story "The Bear" is a good example of an initiation rite told in story form. Although the story is specific to Faulkner's own experience — the young man who is taken out in the wilderness and taught how to hunt — it spotlights the process of growing up. You don't need to hunt or come from that part of the country to enjoy and identify with the young boy. The experiences of our lives differ, but their emotions resonate and bind us together.

Fitzgerald, F. Scott: _The Crackup,_ an account of the author's emotional collapse, was written as therapy, and demonstrates persuasively that the bad times in your life will find a sympathetic ear, and more than that can be an important resource for others in torment.

Gibson, William: _The Seesaw Log_ is a memoir of a project, the play _Two for the Seesaw,_ that recounts the efforts and frustrations in writing a play and mounting a successful Broadway production. The best revenge is writing about it.

Goodall, Jane: _My Life With Chimpanzees_ was written largely for children but will interest animal lovers of all ages.

Her numerous photographs suggest how well your own snap-shots can illustrate your personal history.

Haley, Alex: *Roots* began a wave of interest in family history in this country. An exciting book, it demonstrates that research can enrich drama rather than dry it up.

Hemingway, Ernest: *A Moveable Feast* can help you dare to be notional and opinionated. In this fascinating account of Paris in the late twenties and thirties, Hemingway never troubled himself to be fair or objective, part of the account's charm.

Herriot, James: Perhaps no author persuades us so well that unpretentiousness and gusto make friends with the reader as *All Creatures Great and Small* and his other delightful books that followed.

Isherwood, Christoper: *My Guru, His Disciple* demonstrates that private religious views, private religious struggles are not embarrassing, instead they interest and inspire even those whose own views differ.

Janovy, John, Jr.: *Keith County Journal* wonderfully illustrates the value of a specialist's perspective of the world about him. This author's particular specialty is parasitology, a most forbidding sounding discipline. Nevertheless, his naturalist's eye and enthusiasm take you with him for an exciting fresh look at the network of life.

Johnson, Osa: *I Married Adventure* contains hints for using your own memories to spotlight the life of someone dear to you.

Keillor, Garrison: *Lake Wobegon Days* is a collection of short stories set in rural Minnesota that aptly illustrates the principles discussed in this book. Everyday hometown life and activities can take on an aura of their own.

Kennedy, Rose: *Times to Remember*. A gallant woman shares her children's childhood. An interesting model for parents who want to write about their children.

Kingston, Maxine Hong: *The Woman Warrior: A Memoir of a Girlhood Among Ghosts* is a wonderful source book for second generation writers. It exemplifies ways of including the ambience and the mythology of family life in their own culture, as well as of personalities, interrelations, and the impact of their new environment.

Lawrence, D.H.: *D.H. Lawrence and New Mexico* provides a delightful guide for writers wishing to focus more on their environment than on their personal lives.

Lawrence, T.E.: *The Seven Pillars of Wisdom* combines the impact of the Moslem on the writer with a rousing good adventure story. Dare to mix and match.

Maugham, Somerset: *The Summing Up* wonderfully illustrates gossip as an art form. Stop being ashamed of your over the fence, at the water cooler chats. Get them down on paper. Beyond that this writer's memoir is a rare and frank repository of the notions and techniques that led him to become one of the most popular storytellers of all time.

McCarthy, Mary: *Memories of a Catholic Girlhood* provides an approach to using your current attitudes to illuminate as well as describe your youthful environment.

Montgomery, M.R.: *Saying Goodbye: A Memoir for Two Fathers* illustrates the potential power of the observer. The parent and child relationship has been written about time and again, but each generation experiences it anew and needs fellowship in its agonies and fresh perspectives. This memoir, treating both father and father-in-law, is especially useful to those who wish to balance unusual combinations in the family constellation.

Moon, William Least Heat: *Blue Highways* provides abundant examples of short travel pieces that combine comments on locale, landscape, and people from a purely personal perspective. Notice that curiosity, an empathetic interest in personality, a feel for community, shape these essays rather than set patterns and form.

Muir, John: This autobiography is an honest account of the harsh pioneer life in Wisonsin in the 1800s. It covers the transition time from his childhood in Scotland to the backbreaking labor of hacking a farm out of the wilderness. This little known part of the great naturalist's life, found only in his autobiography, deals with matters that were mundane to him then but have become marvels to us now and formed the man who later became a founder of the national park system.

Niven, David: *The Moon is a Balloon* is another transitional tale. Told with wit and candor, it relates the actor's early life in England and his experiences in Hollywood.

Parkman, Francis: *The Oregon Trail* is an American naturalist and travel writer's account of his trek from the eastern United States through the Wyoming territory. This important document describes the terrain, the Indians, and the uncluttered beauty of a vanished wilderness we can reach only through his record.

Pepys, Samuel: *Diary,* a record scrupulously kept by a man about town in the 17th century, is filled with the lore of a vanished era, the gossip of a vital time, and the activities of the famous. This is a reading experience that will make you feel good about revealing your feelings, observations, and private mischief more openly.

Pritchett, V.S.: *At Home and Abroad* is a vigorous example of what can be done with travels, pouring research, experience, personal observation, and cogitation into a savory stew.

Roosevelt, Eleanor: Her autobiography is a touching story of a neglected childhood that warms the heart without being self pitying.

Rybczynski, Witold: *The Most Beautiful House in the World,* of course, is the house you make with your own hands. And it will always be so even if you are not, as Rybczynski is, a famous architect. Those of you who have one experience, one small portion of your lives you wish to leave behind in permanent record, look here. You'll see how rich the record can be.

Sartin, May: *The House By the Sea* is a beautiful journal of small events during a critical time. The descriptions of neighbors and friends and the ways in which house, sea, and solitude heal show how moving the minutiae of daily life can be. *At Seventy* and *After the Stroke* deal with the joys and catastrophes of aging and show that the process of aging and the fight against disability make heroic reading.

Sills, Beverly: Don't think your personal problems are downers that should be excluded from your memoir. *Bubbles,* an entertaining memoir of the difficulties of the busy life and private tragedies of a great opera singer, illustrates the bonding quality of openness in writing.

Steinbeck, John: Take heart from *Travels with Charley.* This travel book shows that a memoir can falter, dribble away at the end, and still be a marvelous read. Although not as compelling as his *Sea of Cortez*, *Travels with Charley* charmed thousands of Americans with his adventures with his poodle and jerry-built trailer on a round-the-nation trip.

Stevenson, Robert Louis: *Travels with a Donkey* sounds like a travel book, and in a way it is, but more important this memoir reveals the impressions of a young man at a pivotal moment in his life, when he decides upon his career. You have the opportunity to read Stevenson's prose before it matured with his later successes.

Thomas, Dylan: *A Child's Christmas in Wales* demonstrates that you can go home again. This frankly sentimental book evokes scenes and memories of the poet's childhood, producing a work of mythic proportions.

Thurber, James: *My Life and Hard Times* will give you the confidence to sweep up numerous totally unrelated bits and pieces of memory into one story, tied together not so much by a theme as by your own voice and daring.

Twain, Mark (Samuel L. Clemens): *Life on the Mississippi* illustrates a memoir of a particular time in the writer's life, a time of adventure for him, a time when his love of romance ranged freely.

Updike, John: *Self-consciousness: Memoirs.* When you need to steal, steal from the best.

Welty, Eudora: *One Writer's Beginnings* illustrates a theme memoir, in which she traces the influence of family life, childhood, and adolescence on her profession.

White, E.B.: "Once More to the Lake," from *The Essays of E.B. White,* explores the trail of memory from New York sophisticate to young boy.

Wilkinson, Alec: To be honest, *Moonshine* is not a memoir but a study of a cottage industry. Still, Wilkinson approaches his subject in the spirit of the interviewer and journalist. You go along with him to the stills where bootleg whiskey is being made, you meet those defiant traditionalists who keep alive a stubbornness that goes back to the Whiskey Rebellion of 1791. An account to make you dare to dare.

Wright, Ronald: *Time Among the Maya: Travels in Belize, Guatemala, and Mexico* demonstrates that the trivia of movement mix well with research. Notice that what makes this travel book shine is its writer's gusto. He follows his enthusiasms at a cheerful pace, not worrying whether logic or categorization can keep step.

Yardley, Jonathan: *Our Kind of People: The Story of an American Family* is the guide for those whose interests look outward, more at their surroundings than at themselves. You'll find techniques for weaving strands into an entertaining design.

Young, Cathy: *Growing Up in Moscow* shows what can be done with the first generation experience. The differences between the American way of life and that in other countries can be exciting, heartwarming, and insightful. Your private observances and opinions are worth sharing.

37

Researching Your Roots

American Genealogical Research Institute, The. *How to Trace Your Family Tree: A Complete and Easy to Understand Guide for the Beginner.* This book should be available in your library.

Blockson, Charles L. with Ron Fry. *Black Genealogy*, Englewood Cliffs, NJ: Prentice-Hall, Inc., 1977. This informative book can tell you where to start and how to trace your family back to a specific African Kingdom.

Church of Jesus Christ of Latter-day Saints Genealogical Library, 50 East North Temple Street, Salt Lake City, UT 84150. Has the largest library of its kind in the world. It is very helpful, it will direct you to local sources. All its resources are free and open to the public regardless of faith.

Croom, Emily Anne. *Unpuzzling Your Past: A Basic Guide to Genealogy*, 2nd edition, White Hall, VA: Betterway Publications, Inc., 1989. The most highly regarded genealogy primer in print. Shows how to find your roots by combining the use of living sources with research into public records. Contains a chapter on the use of computers in genealogical research.

Doane, Gilbert H. *Searching for Your Ancestors*, Minneapolis: University of Minnesota Press, 1977.

Draznin, Yaffa. *The Family Historian's Handboook*, New York: Harcourt, Brace, Jovanovich, 1978.

Rottenberg, Dan. *Finding Our Fathers: A Guidebook to the Jewish Genealogy*, New York: Random House, 1977. A valuable and interesting resource. This book shows you how to break through the loss of records in the Holocaust to trace your family through sources in the Church of Jesus Christ of Latter-day Saints and in Israel.

Smith, Jessie Carney, editor. *Ethnic Genealogy, a Research Guide.* This collection of material with a foreword by Alex Haley covers Native American, Asian American, Black American, and Hispanic American sources.

U.S. Department of Health, Education and Welfare, National Center for Health Statistics, 5600 Fishers Lane, Room 8-20, Rockville, MD 20852. Will tell you where to find birth and death records and other vital statistics.

U.S. Government Printing Office, Washington, DC 20402. Ask for pamphlets on where to write for various records.

Index